The Critical Years

The Critical Years

Early Years Development from Conception to 5

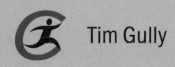 Tim Gully

First published in 2014 by Critical Publishing Ltd.

British Library Cataloguing in Publication Data
A CIP record for this book is available from the British Library

ISBN: 978-1-909330-73-3

This book is also available in the following e-book formats:

MOBI ISBN: 978-1-909330-74-0
EPUB ISBN: 978-1-909330-75-7
Adobe e-book ISBN: 978-1-909330-76-4

The rights of Tim Gully to be identified as the Author of this work have been asserted by him in accordance with the Copyright, Design and Patents Act 1988.

Cover design by Greensplash Limited

Project Management by Out of House Publishing
Typeset by Newgen Knowledge Works Pvt Ltd
Printed and bound in Great Britain by TJ International

Critical Publishing
152 Chester Road
Northwich
CW8 4AL
www.criticalpublishing.com

MIX
Paper from responsible sources
FSC® C013056

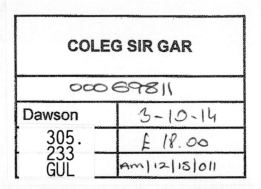

Contents

Acknowledgements

I would like to thank my mother, father and auntie Lil for giving me a safe and happy early childhood. It is the key to everything else.

Meet the author

Tim Gully

Having worked for the Probation Service, the NSPCC and in social work for 25 years, mostly with dangerous offenders and in child protection, Tim made the move into higher education early this century. He has taught both social work and early childhood studies and currently teaches at the University of Chichester. His research interests include the making of children from conception to birth, risk society, social pedagogy and child protection in early years. Working with both victims and abusers, he believes that it is essential to see situations holistically so that we can better understand, intervene and protect children. Internationalism is at the core of his teaching and research and he has been able to teach in Denmark, Romania and Germany, bringing ideas back to include in his teaching in the UK.

Introduction

Learning outcomes:

- to place the child in context;
- to initiate debates to follow, in particular about parenting and risk;
- to consider the role of the practitioner;
- to outline the theoretical child development framework;
- to explain the structure of the book.

Critical question

» *What are the key issues currently facing children in their early years, their parents and carers and the practitioners that work with them?*

I was born an only child to hard-working, middle-class, older parents. We lived in a small town on an island. I remember a tabby cat called Ugi and a blue budgie whose name I have forgotten. I do not remember ever being hungry, especially cold or not having my own room and bed to sleep in. I do remember wanting even more Lego. My mother went back to work when I was about six months old, but not before she had found a wonderful woman to look after me, someone who remained an important person in my life until I had my own children and she was in her nineties. My first school was directly across the road and I remember my time there with affection, even having to do ballet. Theoreticians, I am sure, might make much of the above.

I am here because my parents met, married and decided to try for a child and were successful in this endeavour. They lived in a society in which social expectations, structures and norms were comparatively simple and people could predict how life would go. The world was not unlike that inhabited by previous generations, but things were changing and the rate of change was speeding up. I inherited genes, attitudes and behaviours. I look like my father and have the ectomorphic build of my mother. I support the same football team as my father while my mother taught me to cook and play tennis, activities I continue to enjoy. Both my sons carry the family likeness and physique while my eldest son plays sport and supports the team in blue. My youngest son plays sport, cooks, but to my chagrin supports a different football team because he happened to be born in that city and they were doing better than the blues as he grew up. We are all a link in a chain that stretches back hundreds, if not thousands, of years and stretches forward, in my case, for at least one generation. We inherit a great deal, but also have the ability to grow and make our own choices.

Children in context

Children have always existed but have been seen in society in many different ways, from slaves to gods. Child development that occurs from birth to adulthood was largely ignored throughout much of history. Children were often viewed simply as small versions of adults and little attention was paid to the many advances in the cognitive abilities, language usage and physical growth that take place during childhood and adolescence. Interest in the field of child development finally began to emerge late in the nineteenth century and gathered momentum through the twentieth century, but in these early explorations it tended to focus on abnormal behaviour and how to control and contain the unruly child. Eventually, researchers became increasingly interested in other topics, including typical child development as well as the parental, social and environmental influences on development.

Once upon a time early years development began at birth, but science intervened and we now understand that child development begins at conception and even before. The birth of the first IVF baby, Louise Brown, in 1978 signalled the changes to come. Science is now able to explain heredity through DNA (deoxyribonucleic acid), the substance in the nucleus that enables cells to reproduce and transmit characteristics from generation to generation, and so pass features from parents to offspring. Amongst other things we came to understand development within the womb, but few predicted how dramatic or speedy those changes would be. Concepts of what is 'natural' are routinely challenged with each scientific development while ethical debate, legislation and policy and procedures lag behind.

Betty and Bill Gully did a reasonably good job in rearing me and we might argue that my grandparents did a good job in rearing them, because we are not only talking about genetic heredity here, but also psychological and emotional. If one has been poorly parented as a child one might in turn struggle to understand what is required to be a good parent. This does not mean that adults who have experienced dysfunctional, chaotic or even abusive childhoods cannot become good parents, but they will need luck, support and help to do so. People can change and do so.

Because of biology we can argue that all children are alike, but because of parenting and culture we can also say that no two children are the same. Children differ in physical, psychological, social and emotional growth patterns. Even identical twins, who have the same genetic makeup, are not exactly the same. Think of the children you work with or know. Each is different from the next. While some always appear to be happy, others may not seem as pleasant. Some children are active while others are quiet, even shy and sometimes withdrawn. As practitioners we may struggle to admit that some children are easier to like than others. To help all these children, the practitioner needs to understand the sequence of their development and how development can be influenced by events through the life course. Knowledge of the areas of child development is fundamental to guiding and safeguarding young children. Linked to this is the understanding of healthy brain development, as science has given us the knowledge and understanding of how the body and brain are inter-dependent, working together to create the human child. All children need the support of caring, knowledgeable and skilled adults, be they parents, carers or practitioners. It can be argued that this is especially true of young children, for whom growth and development are happening so fast and who are especially vulnerable.

Parents were once reliant on family to support and advise them, but successive governments have taken an increasing role in providing services and giving advice. Due to child protection, governments have become involved in child rearing through political debate and legislation. There has been a gradual recognition that children should no longer be sent up chimneys to clean them as during the eighteenth and nineteenth centuries, or suffer harm at the hands of parents or carers as highlighted by recent tragic child deaths. The danger is that parenting and child rearing become an obsession for policymakers. Problems that were once associated with the failures of society are increasingly blamed on parents, such as poor achievement at school, drug-taking, obesity, crime and mental health problems. Governments have seen fit to intervene more and more, to be prescriptive, and this trend has been allied to the increase in the number of media experts. On a more positive note, during the twentieth century global organisations such as the United Nations began to take an interest in child welfare and improve the circumstances of millions of children, lifting them out of poverty and providing hope where there was none.

Parenting and the risk society

Wherever on the planet we come from, in some form or another we all have parents, but science and social changes have made it more difficult to clearly define exactly what a parent is there for. Gone are the days when parents were a man and a woman in a marital relationship. We have quite rightly come to accept single parents, same-gender parents and carers in the parenting role. Even in child creation science has played with the role of parent; for instance, is an anonymous sperm donor a parent? In a society where the nature of being a parent is so varied I would argue that the role of the early years practitioner becomes even more important for the development of the child. The practitioner may become the only consistent adult in the life of a child. We need to debate the concept of 'practitioner love' and the notion that practitioners might be seen as replacing parents both physically and emotionally.

Critical question

»   *In the baby rooms of nurseries I have seen practitioners kiss the babies. Do you feel this is appropriate?*

In one sense, of course, the practitioner does replace the parent. The very fact that a parent takes a child to a childminder or nursery means that this replacement is taking place. Indeed, separation is necessary if a child is to begin to develop independence, experience change, develop socially and build resilience, but there are tensions: a danger that parents will be scapegoated for leaving a baby in a baby room perhaps as young as two weeks old, concerns that practitioners 'know best' and that the government is setting standards against which children and parents are being judged.

The politicisation of parenting can have destructive outcomes. The constant labelling of parenting as some kind of problem undermines the confidence of mothers and fathers. Although dysfunctional parents are very much in a minority, the message that is often communicated is about the problems rather than the positives of child rearing and it has a disorienting impact on everybody. Consider for instance the debates on MMR or breast-feeding. Consequently, the numerous initiatives designed to support parents do anything but reassure us – they simply encourage the public to become even more paranoid about parenting. The second outcome of the child rearing debate is that it has intensified the sense of insecurity and anxiety about children's lives and experiences. Society has become obsessed with risk.

The early years should be a time for developing, learning and exploring, but the idea that young children are too vulnerable to be allowed to take risks has become entrenched. How would a parent feel to see a patch of unguarded stinging nettles in the outside play area of a nursery? In Britain, of course, these would probably be chopped down immediately, poisoned and concreted over, but is that the right thing to do? During teaching trips to Denmark I have visited several kindergartens and been very pleased to see nettles and blackthorn in the gardens where children could sting and prick themselves and so learn to be careful around such things. I have seen children cooking with sharp knives close to lighted candles. How wonderful to be free of health and safety and our risk-obsessed society. We, in this country, are far too protective. While we need to reduce significant risk to an acceptable level, we also need to recognise that risks and risk-taking is beneficial. Protecting children from harm, however, should only be a small part of a parent's role. Playing, exploring and stimulating the child are far more important.

There is no doubt that some adults present a serious threat to children. Most of these adults exist within the family, with a very small number of strangers presenting any significant risk. Unfortunately, the media has promoted a sense of paranoia in relation to many aspects of children's lives, and government and professional organisations have fed on this populist view. When children are overly protected from risks, they miss out on important opportunities to learn sound judgement and build their confidence and resilience, for instance when travelling to school. The promotion of suspicion towards adult behaviour seriously undermines the ability of people, especially men, to have a constructive role in the socialisation of babies, toddlers and young children in general. Early years professions have a major problem when it comes to recruiting young men to work in nurseries, primary schools and childcare social work. One reason is the comparatively poor pay, but another has to be acknowledged as the public concern about men and children.

The role of the practitioner partnerships with parents

Practitioners working with the early years, be they nursery workers, health visitors, reception teachers or social workers, have a vital role to play in supporting, and on occasion protecting, young children. The value of the early years practitioner should not be underestimated. While government policy and local procedures may change, and tragedy and enquiry may influence public opinion, the fundamentals of childcare remain the same. Children in their early years need love, physical care, play and stimulation if they are to develop positively as children and into adulthood.

The roles and expectations of the practitioner have increased as children have become the object of unprecedented concern. Anxiety as to whether contemporary families can provide a sufficiently stable setting for children's healthy development is matched by a fear of the risks the child may be at in the wider community. We have a child protection industry that continues to grow. Politicians, policymakers and the child protection 'experts' appear less and less inhibited about lecturing parents on their numerous failings. Practitioners are expected to fill the void that parents may or may not be failing to fill.

It is true that childcare practitioners have an active part to play in safeguarding and managing risk. Risk management is ideally about reducing hazards/threats while increasing benefits. We cannot permanently separate the hazard/threat from the vulnerable object or person. It is impossible to eliminate risk, and indeed all children have to experience risk if they are going to be able to develop resilience and learn to manage themselves with safety, and early years practitioners are in a position to challenge stereotypical views of risk. We can work with parents to challenge it by encouraging children to develop a positive attitude towards the real, not sanitised, outdoors and the adult world. Most important of all, we can challenge it by working together in partnership with parents as active collaborators committed to providing more opportunities for children to explore their world and develop as human beings.

The main aim of any practitioner should be to help the child develop fully to their potential. To do this, early years practitioners need to be trained and supervised. They need to have a set of essential skills. Observing the child is a first step, but we need to place the child in the context in which it is growing and developing. While practitioners will observe and talk to children when assessing them, they will also need to get to know the families if they are to obtain an overall picture of a particular child. Indeed, working in partnership with parents and families is essential not only when it comes to getting to know a particular child, but also when wanting to do new things such as growing that patch of nettles in the outside play area or talking about diverse families. When children are observed, they may be very different from usual. At home, relaxed and with family members, children can be quite different. This can mean that a child who appears to be very quiet at school is talkative and active at home. These observations will feed the assessment so that the child can be given the very best support and opportunities available.

As already described, I have conscious memories of being a child, of generally happy, safe times that undoubtedly influenced my life course to this point and have influenced the content of this book. There will also be unconscious memories. Having once been a child can be both a strength and a hindrance to practitioners working with the early years. Inevitably we are influenced by our past experiences. For instance, when I observe and assess children I have no personal experience of being a sibling. I was a singleton. To enable me to observe and assess objectively I need to recognise this limitation, reflect and make use of the theory and my previous research experience as a practitioner to help provide an understanding of what I am seeing. So becoming a reflective practitioner is vitally important to anyone working as a child-centred welfare practitioner. To do this effectively we need a theoretical framework in which to work.

Theoretical framework

It is vitally important for all practitioners working with young children that they have a developmental framework with which to work and against which to observe and assess. This does not have to be rigid, indeed it should not be. It is crucial that any framework is flexible enough to accommodate not only differing theories, but also different children. An understanding of child development is essential because it allows us to fully appreciate the cognitive, emotional, physical, social and educational growth that children go through from birth into early adulthood. Some of the major theories of child development attempt to describe every aspect of development. These may be based on developmental stages (eg Piaget), or psychodynamic processes (eg Freud). Whatever one's feelings about either of these, every theory has its place and there is a place for every theory. Others might be seen as micro theories, focusing on a limited aspect of child development (eg Bowlby and attachment).

All practitioners need to have access to and an understanding of theory, but they also need to have a critical understanding of this theory and how it might be used. To simply read and believe slavishly is not good enough. Theory is there to help us understand how children grow from conception to adulthood and explains why and how development unfolds. It presents us with models, typologies and sets of ideas that compete for our attention. Some have been around for decades, others are more recent, and it is important not to dismiss either, but rather to draw upon both to create our own personal paradigm of understanding. Once we have done this we must be willing to allow new research and knowledge to influence and change our views. Indeed we are all researchers in our own right. As we build our experience there is a sense that we develop from practitioner into a research practitioner, not only learning, but translating our learning into practice. This does not mean we carry out formal research, although I believe this should be encouraged at all levels, but rather that we build and expand our own knowledge and experience.

Theory therefore is key to our framework, it provides the scaffolding in and around which we work and there will be much of it to come in this book. Practitioners will use their observation and assessment skills and their theoretical knowledge to know not only when they should intervene to help or protect a child, but also when not to intervene. Unnecessary intervention can be as damaging as not intervening when required, but this can present the practitioner with a dilemma. Failing to intervene can lead to tragic consequences, as we have seen with Victoria Climbié, Peter Connelly, Khyra Ishaq, Daniel Pelka and Hamzah Khan. In each of these cases practitioners failed to act. On the other hand, practitioners worry about getting it wrong and reporting something that may turn out to be unfounded, and the impact this would have on the family and on them as practitioners.

In theoretical terms, three of the key themes we will be examining are:

1. Continuity versus discontinuity: whether child development is fluid and gradual or whether it occurs in stages that are prescribed and predictable. How much do a

child's early experiences influence their future? Can we predict a child's future from its upbringing?

2.   The active child versus the passive one: can individual children influence their own development through behaviour (active), or are they at the mercy of their environment (passive)? How much control do children have in a biological and psychological sense over their own development, or are there predictable givens?

3.   Nature v nurture, or more importantly nature via nurture: exploring how development is influenced by our innate biology and genetics (nature) yet moulded by our experiences (nurture). How influential are genes? How influential is parenting? Or are they complimentary?

We will continually return to the notion of child development in relation to parenting and examine the impact it may or may not have upon the development of the child, and within this we will consider the choices that parents have.

Conclusion

In some respects it does appear that having children and child rearing have become more complicated than they once were. While it is true that innovation and social freedom more or less mean that anyone can have a child, we have removed some of the certainty from life and placed parents and practitioners under greater pressure to 'do the right thing'.

One thing I have done deliberately in this chapter, and will continue to do, is use the word 'practitioner' rather than 'professional'. I believe that the word 'professional' implies and creates a gap of expertise between workers and parents, when what we want to do is narrow the gap and create a partnership. The word 'practitioner' also implies what we should be doing and that is working with, getting down on the floor with, playing with children and not remaining aloof observers. 'Practitioner' is for me an action word that reflects what all of us working with children in the early years should be doing.

This has been a brief introduction to some of the themes this book will discuss and some of the controversies that are currently debated. I have placed the child in context, touched upon the roles of the parent and practitioner and reminded the reader of the essential place that theory and research should take within practice.

Finally, as I have grown older I have come more and more to appreciate the job that my parents and 'Auntie' Lil did in supporting and guiding me, especially since becoming a parent myself. Working in childcare has further allowed me to reflect on how my upbringing influences me as a practitioner and how important it is to have the scaffolding of experience and developmental theory to keep me, my colleagues and the children I work with safe.

Structure of the book

The book is very much written with the child and practitioner or parent in mind. It follows a simple structure, following the child along the life course through physical growth, psychological development and social expansion. It considers how children can be impacted upon by disability and abuse. It is designed to be read from beginning to end or dipped into as needed.

Taking it further

Becket, C and Taylor, H (2010) *Human Growth and Development*. London: SAGE.

Daniel, B, Wassell, S and Gilligan, R (2010) *Child Development for Child Care and Protection Workers*. London: Jessica Kingsley.

Furedi, F (2008) *Paranoid Parenting*. London: Continuum.

Horwath, J (2010) *The Child's World*. London: Jessica Kingsley.

Lindon, J (2012) *Understanding Child Development 0–8 Years*. London: Hodder Education.

Mukherji, P and Dryden, L (eds) (2014) *Foundations of Early Childhood*. London: SAGE.

Page, J, Clare, A and Nutbrown, C (2013) *Working with Babies and Children*. London: SAGE.

Wilkinson, I (2010) *Risk Vulnerability and Everyday Life*. London: Routledge.

1 Foetal development

Learning outcomes:

• to understand embryo and foetal growth from conception to birth;

• to explore scientific and legal developments in relation to pregnancy;

• to identify negative parental behaviours that may shape the foetus in the womb;

• to examine the role of parental choice;

• to recognise social influences on conception and pregnancy.

Critical questions

» *Scientific advances have greatly increased our understanding of foetal development and brought a level of maternal and paternal control over outcomes. Is there a danger we may take this too far?*

» *Why do we have babies?*

Introduction

Many texts will begin child development at birth, when in fact it begins at conception. The word 'birth' conjures up a miraculous event that should be exciting for the mother, father and wider family (Becket and Taylor, 2010, Chapter 1). The significance of it cannot be underestimated, nor the risks for the mother and baby ignored, but this all begins long before. One can argue that in fact child development begins even earlier with the decision of two people, bringing with them their genetic coding and parental potential, to couple and reproduce. In most cases people will make choices about whom they have sex with and certainly plan to have children with. Fundamental drivers such as desire and attraction play their part, but as the relationship develops, cognitive skills also come into play in assessing the partner and potential partnership. This said, in some cases pregnancy is an 'accident' or people do not think through whom they are having children with, they do not look forward or think about consequences, but then why should they? They may be in love and most people believe in a happy ever after.

Brief relationships can lead to pregnancy, but generally when two people meet and plan a future together they will probably have found some common beliefs such as religion, social or sporting activities, enjoyable, compatible sex, friendship groups and so forth. There is likely to have been discussion about having children and how many or indeed agreement about not having any. If couples have significant differences they will probably not stay together. This pre-selection activity is good for the future child or children of the relationship, making good parenting and successful child rearing more likely. This is not to say, however, that relationships that begin well with a good foundation will not founder and see children suffer emotional or physical trauma, but the likelihood of a good outcome is increased. This suggests that having a successful parenting couple, rather than a single parent, is better for the child, something that is patently not true. The child needs good parenting and this is as likely to come from a single parent or gay couple as it is from the traditional husband and wife. It is interesting to note that some women are now deciding to do without a partner and buy sperm directly from the internet. The debate on the impact of this decision on the child is still to be had, but it does take away the relationship-building phase, the sharing of hopes and dreams and nest-building.

Critical questions

» *Is having a child by a sperm donor any different from a one night stand and/or becoming a single parent after a relationship breakdown?*

» *How might it affect the child as he or she grows up?*

Genetic background

However the child is conceived it will be the result of two sets of genes coming together. The cells of all living beings contain DNA, the substance in the nucleus that enables cells to reproduce and transmit characteristics from generation to generation. This partly explains why we look like our parents and grandparents and why we behave and think in the way we do as mammals. It also explains why every individual is different, but also the same wherever they are from on the planet. DNA is both an individual and a species code, although we do in fact share 99% of the DNA of apes (Ridley, 2003, 24). The other factor that influences how we are is nurture, and we will look at the relationship nature and nurture have, and how the two work together to form a human being.

When cells divide, the DNA takes the form of chromosomes, carrying the genes that pass hereditary features from parents to offspring. Different species of mammals have varying numbers of chromosomes per cell. Human body cells normally contain 46 distinctive chromosomes, with 23 from the egg and 23 from the sperm cell coming together at fertilisation to create a fresh, unique combination of genes. Sperm and ovum are termed 'gametes' (from the Greek meaning 'marriage partners'). When they 'marry' they basically make one completely new cell – the human embryo, or zygote.

At fertilisation this embryo is about 0.1mm in diameter. Since characteristics come from both parents the zygote is never the same as, or part of, the mother, but is a genetically distinct individual. The mother is basically a host. The colouring of the hair, skin and eyes, the sex of the new human being, and factors influencing height and build, are determined at fertilisation by information in the DNA but, as we will discuss in this chapter, even these natural traits are open to scientific manipulation and change.

Critical questions

»   Is scientific progress in respect of our understanding of genetics good for us?

»   What are the positives and negatives of scientific 'progress'?

Over the last ten years DNA testing has become popular. Depending on the type of relationship to be tested those involved will submit samples of their DNA collected using cheek swabs. For example, if a paternity test is needed a sample will also be collected from the child in question, the alleged father and the mother. Once collected, the samples will be submitted to a DNA testing laboratory for detailed analysis. The laboratory will then compare specific locations on the DNA to determine whether or not there is a biological relationship.

Foetal growth and development in pregnancy

So two people have come together, whether planned, accidentally or virtually, but they have done enough to conceive and the journey begins towards becoming an adult: *An adult human consists of over a million million cells* (Davies, 2014, p 17). The human egg is always female until it comes into contact with the semen of the male and so a child's gender is determined at fertilisation (Ridley, 2003). A chromosome from the father's sperm determines whether the child is male or female. If an X chromosome is present the baby is a girl and if a Y chromosome is carried by the sperm instead it is a boy. This is natural selection as it has always been, but science is now able to influence gender choice. In the early weeks of pregnancy, the developing baby is called an embryo and then, from about eight weeks onward, it is called a foetus.

It is approximately three weeks from the first day of the woman's last menstrual period that the fertilised egg moves gradually along the fallopian tube towards the womb. Occasionally two eggs are released by the ovary and fertilised. This results in fraternal twins who are different in appearance and may be of different gender because their genes form from two eggs and two sperm cells. Rarely, one embryo splits into two and both cells develop separately, as with identical twins. The egg begins as one single cell, but while in the fallopian tube the cell divides repeatedly so that by the time the egg reaches the womb it has become a mass of over 100 cells and is still growing (Davies, 2014).

The genes that are passed down through the family – that is, are inherited – can change and become faulty. The faulty gene may cause a disorder, which can affect growth, development or health. Many of the health or developmental problems seen at birth are directly due to either a fault in the genetic information or to a combination of the inherited genetic information and environmental causes, such as diet, chemical exposure and lifestyle. Some genetic disorders may not be noticed until later in childhood, adolescence or adulthood. It is at this very early stage that heritable and chromosomal disorders are already present.

CASE STUDY

Amanda

Amanda was 6 pounds when she was born and she initially had difficulty putting on weight. After a spell in hospital when she was suffering from bronchitis it was thought that she had asthma, but her mother Jenny, who was a nurse, was already beginning to suspect that Amanda had cystic fibrosis. On the one hand, with no history of the condition in either her family or her husband's, this seemed impossible – but there was no other explanation of the symptoms that Amanda was displaying. Eventually, she was given a sweat test and it was confirmed that she did have cystic fibrosis. Following tests it was confirmed that both Jenny and Simon were carriers – which is how they unknowingly passed on the faulty cystic fibrosis gene to Amanda. Jenny blamed herself and in conversations with a social worker said that she wished she had never had a child.

Scientific and medical progress are allowing us to take some control over these events, giving parents the opportunity to make decisions.

Critical reflection

At the time of writing the technique known as 'three-parent IVF' came a step closer after the Department of Health asked the fertility regulator to conduct a public consultation into its ethical acceptability. At the same time, the Wellcome Trust announced extra funds to expand research into the technique, which involves using genetic material from three parents – two women and a man – to create a baby. The procedure, currently illegal in the UK, is aimed at helping the estimated 12,000 people who are living with mitochondrial disease, which is a defect in the small structures called mitochondria that surround the cell nucleus. The disease is inherited but is only passed down through the maternal line. About 100 babies are born each year with a severe form of the disease, for which there is no cure, with many dying in infancy.

The proposed procedure involves removing the nucleus from an affected woman's egg, transferring it to the shell of an egg provided by a female donor who has healthy mitochondria, and then fertilising it with the sperm of the affected woman's partner. The resulting baby would have genetic characteristics chiefly from its mother and father plus some from the mitochondria of its third parent, who provided the donor egg.

» *How do you feel about this?*

» *If Jenny had had access to the knowledge that Amanda was going to be born with a disability might she have had her aborted?*

Embryo arrives in the womb

The embryo literally burrows into the womb lining and the outer cells reach out like roots to link with the mother's blood supply. The inner cells form into two and then later three layers. Each of these layers will grow to be different parts of the baby's body with the first layer becoming the brain and nervous system, the skin, eyes and ears. The second layer becomes the lungs, stomach and gut while the third layer becomes the heart, blood, muscles and bones. This all happens before the end of the fifth week of pregnancy and the time of the first missed period when many women are only just beginning to think they might be pregnant. Inside the womb the baby floats in a bag of fluid called the amniotic sac. It is this sac that will break when the baby is ready to be born.

At this stage, the foetal nervous system is starting to develop as a hollow tube from the top layer of cells that will become the brain and spinal cord. Defects in this tube are the cause of spina bifida, a condition where the spine does not fully close. The exact causes are unknown, but several risk factors have been identified, the most significant being a lack of folic acid before and at the very start of pregnancy. This has led to folic acid being prescribed to pregnant mothers and to some debate as to the possibility of adding folic acid to all bread. Here we have an example of government making health decisions that may seem to be in the best interests of the unborn child, but take away parental choice, unless of course you make your own bread.

As the tube is forming so is the heart. A string of blood vessels from the heart to the mother will become the umbilical cord. The head is growing as the brain develops and the heart can already be seen beating on an ultrasound scan. At approximately the same time indents are clearly visible on the side of the head, which will become the ears, and there are thickenings where the eyes will be. On the body limb buds are forming and show where the arms and legs are growing. By now, at approximately seven weeks, the embryo has increased to about 10mm long from head to toe. An ultrasound will show a face is slowly forming and the eyes are more obvious and have some colour in them. There will be a mouth with a tongue. There are now the beginnings of hands and feet, with ridges from where the fingers and toes will develop. The major internal organs are all developing apace (Davies, 2014).

At nine weeks, the baby has grown to about 22mm long and the relationship between mother and baby is normally now well advanced. Biologically the baby is totally dependent on the host and a psychological relationship is also taking shape. This will, of course, depend on the attitude of the mother and father towards the baby. We know that this relationship is complex and will influence the future for the baby, mother and father.

While the psychological relationship is complex, the biological one is more straightforward and based on predictable stages. The placenta is rooted to the lining of the womb and separates the baby's circulation from the mother's. In the placenta, oxygen and food from the mother's bloodstream pass across into the baby's bloodstream and are carried to the baby along the umbilical cord. Antibodies, giving resistance to infection, pass from mother to baby to begin to establish its immune system. The umbilical cord is literally the baby's lifeline, the link between baby and mother, and as we will see in the coming pages, as well as carrying so much goodness it can carry harmful and often toxic substances that may cause the unborn harm while still in the womb, such as excessive alcohol and drugs. In the case of twins or larger multiple births each child will have their own umbilical cord that does not get tangled, because every embryo is contained in the mother's uterus as a separate unit. All placental mammals have the umbilical cord, the essential conduit allowing blood to circulate, carrying oxygen and food to the baby and carrying waste away, and for this reason we all have a naval (belly button) or a simple scar, proof that we were all once a foetus in a womb (Davies, 2014).

Critical reflection

When did you last look at your belly button? Do so now and think about how it was once one end of an umbilical cord connecting you to your mother. How does that make you feel?

Thirteen weeks to 40 weeks

This stage of foetal growth is known as the second trimester. At about 12 weeks after conception the foetus is fully formed. It has all its organs, muscles, limbs and bones (apart from the knee caps which do not fully form until after birth in order to ease giving birth), and its sexual organs are well developed. The baby is already moving about, but the movements cannot yet be felt by the mother. Longitudinal growth is now pronounced and at 14 weeks the baby is about 85mm long from head to bottom. Remarkably, when you think how much the baby has developed, the pregnancy may be just beginning to show, but this varies a lot from woman to woman. The baby is now growing quickly. The body of the baby grows bigger so that the head and body are more in proportion. The face begins to look much more human and the hair is beginning to grow as well as eyebrows and eyelashes. The eyelids stay closed over the eyes. The lines on the skin of the fingers are now formed, so the baby already has its own individual fingerprint. Finger and toenails are growing and the baby has a firm handgrip.

At about 20 weeks the mother may feel the baby move. The baby is now moving about vigorously and responds to touch and sound. At 24 weeks (the maximum age at which British law allows for elective abortion) the baby is 'viable', meaning that the baby is now thought to have a chance of survival if born. Most babies born before this time struggle to survive, but the care that can now be given in neonatal units means that more and more babies born early do survive even as young as 18 weeks, when it would fit neatly in an adult hand. At around 26 weeks the baby's eyelids open for the first time. When babies are born their eye colour is normally blue, sometimes black or brown, and it is not until some weeks after birth that the eyes become the colour they will stay. The head-to-bottom length at 30 weeks is about 33cm.

Once beyond 28 weeks mother and baby have entered the third trimester that will continue until the baby is born at approximately 40 weeks. While the baby will continue to grow and develop the mother will experience significant changes to her own body that may include swelling of the ankles and fingers, tender breasts, which may leak a watery pre-milk called colostrum, trouble sleeping, and the baby dropping, or moving down lower in the abdomen.

Science and the unborn child

There is much talk within the media about 'designer children' and it is true that science can now help parents pick what gender they want their child to be, what eye and hair colour they want it to have. We talk of saviour children, of having a child to save another and, as we have seen with three-parent IVF, science now has the potential to treat for potential disability. In Britain such decisions are limited by the 2008 Human Fertilisation and Embryology Act. The ethical and moral issues are complex and while the law attempts to regulate these one cannot ignore the difference science has made in a very short space of time and the public demand for these services.

Becoming pregnant, carrying the unborn and giving birth was once, not that long ago, a comparatively straightforward process. Parents could either have or not have children. Biology and, for some, gods made the decisions for you and there was no other option but to either remain childless or adopt. Since the birth of Louise Brown, the first IVF baby (where fertilisation takes place in a dish, 'in vitro') in 1978 things have changed dramatically. Four per cent of all children born in the UK are now IVF babies, surrogacy is accepted, self-fertilisation is available and you can leave the UK to undertake treatments abroad to model the baby you want. Is it so bad to be able to determine a child's hair colour or gender?

We have advanced so fast we have gone beyond considering what is available locally and with the rapid growth of the global society not only has childhood changed irreversibly, but so has parenting and for many the child has become the must-have accessory. Obsessed with our own youth and wanting perfect, intelligent children who live in a world of designer clothes and toys, we now have the means to meet our desires. Be it a child brought from the slums of the developing world for adoption or a child created through science in the womb, we can have the child of our choice.

> Welcome to Fertility 1st. You have taken the first steps towards letting us help you try to fulfil your dreams of having the baby you have longed for. We offer women a life changing opportunity towards motherhood with our anonymous and extensive sperm donor database. We provide the donor introduction for you and then show you how simple the arrangement can be by enabling you to book your own delivery and testing of both yourself and your donor.
>
> (www.fertilityfirst.com.au, 12 April 2008)

Fertility 1st is but one of many companies offering this type of service while others go further, offering genetic modification. As Fertility 1st's website puts it: The Best of Nature before you Nurture.

In the light of these developments, adoption rates are falling year on year and more hard-to-place children are being left in the care system. At the time of writing there were 56,000 children, the population of a small town, in children's homes and in long-term foster care in the UK with little hope of being moved on to family life. A majority of prospective adopters want healthy, 'normal' babies and if adoption does not have what they want or is too slow in providing it, there are now plenty of options for getting what they want. It is interesting to note that in 2008 the Indian Government legalised commercial surrogacy with the introduction into law of the

Assisted Reproductive Technology (Regulation) Act. In the UK you can pay reasonable expenses to a surrogate but it is illegal to pay her a fee. The Indian Government had recognised that the trade needed regulating, but also that the potential for earning foreign currency from wombing foreign foetuses was significant with an estimated annual earning potential of £250 million.

Risks to the unborn child

The unborn child grows from fertilised egg to foetus to a child ready to be born within the womb and is totally dependent upon the host for all it needs. The relationship between mother and child is being influenced and changed. During pregnancy not only does the baby develop, but the mother physically and emotionally changes and her relationship with her partner, friends and family may also change because of it. These changes influence how the child will be nurtured. In most pregnancies the mother is a safe, caring host protecting the unborn as she will when it is born and grows up. In some cases, however, the mother is far from responsible or does not understand the risks that her behaviour can cause. I have mentioned the umbilical cord and how essential it is. It is like a highway carrying essential products in and waste out, but sometimes it will carry toxic waste in. In this section we will consider the risks of parental harm to the baby.

Abortion

Ethics and morality are further brought into sharp focus by the abortion debate. In England, Wales and Scotland the law is comparatively simple with any woman legally able to terminate a pregnancy up to 24 weeks and beyond with extenuating medical circumstances. These rules are contained within the 2008 Human Fertilisation and Embryology Act. Ironic that an act of Parliament that opens up new vistas on creating life should also sanction the destruction of life. There is no intention here, however, to get into that debate in terms of rights and wrongs as individuals will have their own view of the subject, but it is important that we consider and understand the issues and the intense dilemmas that women face when making these decisions.

Critical reflection

As practitioners working within the early years we are expected to remain objective when working with all parents whatever their gender, religion, social, economic and ethical outlook.

» *As a practitioner, how do you balance your own ethical and moral outlook with contradictory views held by colleagues or parents? Would you be happy to challenge these?*

It is interesting to note that the unborn under British law has few rights. Criminal law does not allow for the murder or manslaughter charge to be brought against anyone that kills a foetus; indeed how could we have abortion if it did? Anyone killing a foetus is likely to be charged with foetal destruction. In legal terms the child really does not exist until it is actually born. Social workers, for instance, cannot get a court order to protect the child until it is born and I have vivid memories of removing a 19-minute-old child from its mother under police powers with a uniformed police officer at my side. It was not a good experience for any of us, but the welfare of the child is paramount and the newborn was deemed to be at immediate risk of harm.

Whatever our ethical views are about the benefits or otherwise of scientific developments and the law there is general agreement about the damage that can be done to the foetus through abuse during pregnancy, be it from domestic violence, drug or alcohol misuse, stress or lack of nourishment.

The first two are perhaps more obvious but the second two are less so. The exposure to stress releases the stress hormone cortisol that, like drugs, will cross the placenta and may cause the baby to be stressed as they grow. Children that are born having experienced stress in the womb may well become stressed and agitated in their early years and later. There might well be connections here with such things as ADHD. Nourishment is simple in that for foetal development the mother needs to eat a balanced diet so that the growing baby gets the nutrients it needs to grow. Both of these highlight further the link between maternal well-being and foetal well-being.

Inevitably, whatever the lifestyle of the mother, the baby can be affected by any particular negative behaviour she might decide to follow or experience. The mother as the host is given the responsibility to care for the life growing within her and society expects her to make child-focused decisions, something that is not helped by the often confusing advice given by the government, media experts or professionals. While we generally accept that using drugs, legal or illegal, during pregnancy can have a detrimental impact upon the unborn the view on drinking alcohol is less clear. Is a glass of wine each day really so prejudicial to the health of the unborn?

Alcohol and drug dependency

Parental alcohol misuse can cause harm *from conception through to adulthood* (Horwath, 2010, 336). We do know that Foetal Alcohol Syndrome (FAS), for which there is no current treatment, is a serious condition. It is the most common cause of non-genetic mental damage in Western society and can induce symptoms such as:

* abnormal facial features;

* reduced growth;

* central nervous system abnormalities;

* impaired learning and memory skills;

* behavioural problems such as hyperactivity.

FAS is caused by alcohol disrupting the formation and survival of nerve cells in the foetus' developing brain, particularly in the final three months of pregnancy and the first few years after birth when brain development is particularly active.

A woman's drug use can affect both her foetus and her newborn. Most drugs cross the placenta – the organ that provides nourishment to the foetus. Some can cause direct toxic (poisonous) effects and drug dependency in the foetus. After birth, some drugs can be passed to the baby through breastfeeding.

CASE STUDY

Stephanie

Stephanie was born prematurely with neonatal withdrawal syndrome. The hospital contacted social services and I remember standing beside the incubator watching this small pink creature twitching from the effects of the heroin her mother had used on a regular basis before and during pregnancy. Stephanie was being treated with a small dosage of morphine every four hours and the nursing staff were optimistic. On this occasion they were right to be as two weeks later Stephanie left hospital with her foster parents. Many children suffering from neonatal withdrawal syndrome are not so lucky, with the risk of complex congenital problems arising including impact on brain development.

Substance misuse may affect parenting through childhood and into adolescence. Inevitably it can lead to failings in basic safe care and will leave children in the early years especially vulnerable, and yet even young children will develop coping strategies when living with substance abuse. This is something we will look at in greater depth in later chapters. We must also remain objective and remember that substance abuse in itself does not make someone a bad parent.

Critical reflection

Judges in family courts generally take the view that we should not negatively judge a parent for misusing substances, but rather consider the impact the misuse has on parenting.

» *I have met many good parents who successfully manage their habit. What do you think?*

Domestic violence

Accepting for the moment that there is an element of choice even in addiction with drug and alcohol misuse, there may be little choice when experiencing domestic violence. It is difficult enough for a victim of domestic violence to escape, but pregnancy brings with it further vulnerability and also complex emotions of hope that *things might get better*. The consequences of a woman experiencing domestic violence during pregnancy can be very serious. Blows to the abdomen may lead to miscarriage and stillbirth and repeated physical abuse can result in foetal fractures, maternal and foetal haemorrhage, rupture of the uterus, liver or spleen, premature separation of the placenta, or premature delivery of the foetus. Pregnant women in violent relationships have an increased risk of low birth weight. We also have to remember that the term 'domestic violence' does not only cover the use of physical force, but also involves emotional abuse and control. This may cause stress that, as has already been explained, can have an impact on the unborn child (Horwath, 2010, Chapter 19).

Conclusion

Medicine and science have removed many of the uncertainties from conception, pregnancy and birth, although in fact these uncertainties were in themselves certainties. You could either have or not have a child and how that child appeared physically was down to how the mother and her partner looked. Birth would probably happen in hospital or maybe at home and parents would follow the advice of the professionals involved. There was a time when medical and nursing staff always knew best. The idea of choice was hardly there at all, and if there was choice it would be very limited. The birth of Louise Brown and the arrival of the internet changed everything and now perhaps we have too much information and too many choices. A woman no longer needs a man to impregnate her, you can literally design your own baby and the discovery of DNA gives us the opportunity to eradicate genetic defects and disability. We are indeed entering a brave new world.

Summary

In this chapter we have examined the growth of the foetus in the womb, the dangers it faces and the choices that parents have from before birth and during pregnancy. In so doing we have started to consider our theoretical dilemmas on how the child grows and develops and, in particular, to explore the nature v nurture conundrum that begins at conception if not before. We have examined the growth of the child within the womb and looked at the role science is playing and the influence government policy and media debate have on the decisions parents make.

Critical reflection

» Do you think we have too many choices when it comes to pregnancy and birth?

» Science is suggesting that disability, at least caused genetically and/or in the womb, may soon be eradicated. Is this a good thing?

Taking it further

Take time to research conception choices on the internet and consider where science could be taking us.

Howell, M (2009) Effective Birth Preparation: Your Practical Guide to a Better Birth. Headley Down: Intuition UN Ltd.

References

Becket, C and Taylor, H (2010) Human Growth and Development. London: SAGE.

Davies, J (2014) Life Unfolding: How the Human Body Creates Itself. Oxford: Clarendon Press.

Horwath, J (2010) The Child's World. London: Jessica Kingsley.

Ridley, M (2003) Nature via Nurture. London: Harper.

2 The physical child

Learning outcomes:

- to explore brain development in the early years;
- to consider physical development and motor skills;
- to introduce ideas of well-being and public health in relation to children;
- to examine the role of parents and practitioners and consider social influences;

Critical question

» *What is the relation between the predictable biological stages of growth and the parenting the child receives, the environment in which it lives and government involvement?*

Introduction

So our child is ready to be born and arrives. Apart from the eyes that are fully developed at birth, she will grow and develop at a fast pace during the coming early weeks and months. Predictable changes in physical functioning occur in most children during the first two years. In infancy, survival mechanisms, such as reflexes, are implemented; crying time peaks then decreases, feeding moves from milk to a combination of milk and soft solids, and motor skills permit exploration. Early childhood consists of vigorous physical activity and the acquisition of new motor skills and the development of cognitive understanding and language. In this chapter we will concentrate on physical development from conception to the age of five with reference to well-being and risks to the unborn and infant. There will also be some debate about parental choice in respect to having and rearing the child.

Although each child is unique, the basic patterns, or principles, of growth and development are universal, predictable and orderly. A baby born to the reclusive Arrow People of the Amazon jungle will have the same physical characteristics as a baby born in a modern paediatric unit in Britain. Genetic endowment will influence appearance, but only exposure to culture and life events will physically change the infant and make it different to the next. Genes influence every aspect of human growth, developing a relationship with nurture that will determine not only the physical development of the child, but also every aspect of their coming existence. We should no longer talk about nature v nurture, but rather nature via nurture. The relationship between these two factors can be positive, allowing the child to successfully grow, or negative and limiting because of poor care or abuse. Through careful observation and interaction with children, practitioners understand the characteristics and principles of these and the potential outcomes. Good practitioner assessment is therefore based on an understanding of child development and trained developmental skills.

Birth choices

As the weeks and months of pregnancy go by so we move towards the birth and mothers and fathers have to make decisions. If the pregnancy is going well, by about 32 weeks the baby is usually lying head downwards and is ready for birth. Sometime before birth the head may move down into the pelvis and is said to be engaged, but sometimes the baby's head does not engage until labour has started. As already mentioned, inside the womb the baby floats in the amniotic sac and before or during labour the sac breaks: the mother's waters have broken.

We in Western society generally accept the role of practitioners in advising us and caring for us during pregnancy. In focusing on the art of governing, Michel Foucault originated the concept of 'governmentality' which he defined as the use of resources such as medical care, education, employment, family life and mass media to steer the public into specific values and 'good' behaviours (Rabinow, 1984, p 13). Practitioners, it might be said, are there to govern and direct individuals to certain ends. We can see this in the care provided at birth. Fifty years ago most births took place at home with a midwife in attendance and then maternity units took over with home births greatly decreasing. The concept of choice, especially for women, is a new and powerful one, but the offer of choice can in itself be seen as a means to manage birth.

While most women give birth in a maternity unit, this is not the only option. The midwife should discuss the birth with the mother and the different choices available. In some areas there is greater choice due to the availability of midwifery-led units, and in others the choice is between a home and hospital birth. Elective caesareans have become popular and these have to be done in hospital. Women may also choose a hospital birth if they want to have an epidural when in labour, or to have doctors on hand if they need it. Alternatively, women who choose to have their babies at home report high satisfaction levels through being more in control, while midwifery-led units provide support for a normal birth in a home-from-home environment. The opportunity to labour in water is recommended for pain relief by the National Institute for Health and Clinical Excellence (NICE). An informed choice should be a well-thought-out decision, based on an accurate understanding of the full range of options, the risks and benefits of each option and their possible results. Yet as we have seen, and will continue to see through the course of this book, choices in baby and childcare are not so easy to make, partly for ethical and moral reasons, sometimes because of the wide range of often contradictory advice available and because of practitioner power and control.

The most vulnerable in our society, those without the understanding, support or reflexive ability, are often powerless to make their own informed choices or challenge the decisions of nursing and medical staff. For instance, in a culturally diverse society such as we have in Britain the Western approach to childbirth is not always the most sympathetic.

CASE STUDY

Dotty

Dotty arrived in England from Zimbabwe pregnant and with her young son seeking asylum. Apart from having ongoing contact with immigration she also had regular encounters with nursing and medical staff, and each visit provided lessons in new bodily regimes relevant to the cultivation of Western behavioural traits such as check-ups, vitamins and routine urine and blood tests. While clinicians focused on disciplining Dotty's body to regulate her childbirth, they failed to understand her own cultural values and expectations. This, in essence, devalued her own experience in deference to biomedical authority. Dotty thought the prenatal visits were excessive, a constant invasion of her body, and inferred that something must be wrong with her baby.

Critical question

»   *How can we as practitioners balance the need to meet medical and nursing demands with the social and cultural needs of the child, parents and families?*

Early physical growth

Birth is potentially a dangerous process wherever it takes place, but has become safer over the decades. In most cases the newborn will be successfully delivered and will have all its physical parts apart from its knee caps. Once born development tends to proceed from top to bottom, from the head downward and according to this process the child first gains control of the head, then the arms, then the legs. As we observe the growing baby we will see the baby's limbs will begin to straighten out. At first there appears to be little voluntary control over movement; this is something that will develop over time and we would expect the child to gain control of head and face movements within the first two months after birth.

Our understanding of child development means that we expect babies and children to be able to do certain things within particular time frames. So the infant will be able to lift themselves up using their arms and by 12 months of age infants start to gain leg control and may be able to crawl, stand or even walk. As we observe we will see that development also proceeds from the centre of the body outward and logically, when one remembers how important it is, the spinal cord (remember from the previous chapter how it began as a tube) develops before other parts of the body. The child's arms develop before their hands, and hands and feet develop before fingers and toes.

Predictable changes in physical functioning occur in most children during infancy and it is these we look for when observing and assessing the infant. We expect the child to develop not only physically, but also in respect to survival instincts and awareness. The improving ability to move means that the child begins to explore and starts to learn about its environment. This growing process requires energy and feeding moves from milk to a combination of milk and soft solids, and motor skills permit exploration. So early childhood consists of vigorous physical development and the acquisition of new understanding and skills. Any assessment of a child's development has to be based on outcomes and it has always amazed me how children who suffer the most severe illnesses or abuse can come through to lead successful lives. These orderly changes demonstrate the relationship between the brain and the body. Much of the maturation depends on changes in the brain and the nervous system and these changes assist children to improve their thinking abilities and skills.

Critical reflection

If the opportunity arises to observe a baby's progress into infancy and beyond, take it. There is nothing better for a practitioner's learning than that which comes from observation.

As the child develops, physical skills develop from macro to micro movements. So, for instance, an infant will have unco-ordinated movements to begin with, but within a short time these movements become co-ordinated and the infant can grasp an object. The principles of development help the practitioner understand that the order or sequence of development in children is generally the same and the practitioner can then judge when something is not right. However, each child develops at his or her own rate. In any early years setting, one may find children the same age who have progressed to different levels in each developmental area. Knowing the principles of development will help the practitioner observe what abilities each child has gained.

Because of theorists such as Piaget we have in Western society developed the view that all babies and infants should be reaching approximately the same physical developmental stage or milestone at the same time, and if they do not then there may be something 'wrong' either with the child or with the parenting. Parents have the immediate care of their children, but increasingly it seems that society and institutions determine what our children should be doing and how they should be doing it. To some extent this view is of course true. We know that different systems of the body grow at different rates. All children have certain ingrained targets in physical growth that their bodies aim for. But we also know that these can be temporarily or permanently deterred by illness, abuse or inadequate care. Marginal difference is accepted by practitioners working with the early years, but more significant differences need to be observed, recorded and reported.

The maturation view argues that there is a sequence of changes in the foetus, baby and toddler that are controlled by genetic coding. Indeed the nature v nurture debate has been quite rightly superseded by the view that nature develops via nurture. We recognise genetic inheritance, but also the significant impact that is had by care-giving. So before the child is even conceived parental influence is there, lurking in the background ready to bring with it the positives and negatives, and then as adults we see our mother or father staring back at us from the bathroom mirror.

The brain and its development

The human brain is a remarkably complex organ that regulates basic physiological functions (eg heart rate), sensations of pleasure and pain, motor skills and co-ordination, emotional responses and intellectual processes. It is an organ that we are only beginning to fully understand and neuroscience is taking our understanding ever forward (Becket and Taylor, 2010, pp 56–8). The development of the brain of course begins in the womb and as suggested above can be affected by parental behaviour. At birth, a child's brain weighs about one pound and is underdeveloped, but contains the fundamental, billions of specialised nerve cells called neurons. Although these cells are present at birth, they are not yet linked and it is nature in close conjunction with nurture that does the linking (Ridley, 2003). Once the child is born, and especially during the first 18 months after birth, the brain develops at a faster rate than it ever will again and this period is critical to create a healthy brain capable of serving the person for the rest of their lives.

CASE STUDY

Yon

Yon was born in Bucharest in 1988 to his 14-year-old mother. As was the custom then Yon was given up to the state foster home system. The 1989 Revolution overthrew the Ceausescu regime and Western journalists gained unprecedented access to Romania and quickly discovered the tragic state of the children's homes. Babies are very sensitive to touch, they like the feel of soft fabrics, skin-to-skin contact with their parents and, of course, lots of cuddling, something the Romanian children did not get. A British couple went there in 1990 after watching a television documentary and adopted Yon. Yon demonstrated a lack of affection and struggled to learn. Scans of Yon's brain showed black areas where the circuits had not connected. Unperturbed, his parents focused on providing him with physical and emotional affection in order to try to connect the missing links.

Critical question

» *If you are based in an early years setting, or have experience of one, do you believe we can teach empathy, attachment and resilience?*

Healthy brain development in the early months of life is vitally important (Mukherji and Dryden, 2014, pp 96–7). During the first 18 months of life the brain develops at a very fast pace with each part of the brain connecting to the next like the London Underground map. Imagine it lit up and became alive, sending messages hither and yon. These links, or connections, are called synapses and brain-wiring occurs as new links form. The larger the number of synapses, the greater the number of messages that can be transmitted between the various parts of the brain and the more efficiently the brain can operate. Different areas of the brain control different functions, as follows:

- cerebellum (movement, balance);
- medulla oblongata (controls breathing, heart rate);
- midbrain (vision, movement, hearing);
- limbic system (memory, emotion);
- hypothalamus (regulates body temperature and hunger);
- thalamus (regulates sleep, relays sensory and motor functions);
- cerebrum (language, planning, thought).

Critical reflection

Understanding the areas and principles of development is important. Recognising how the brain functions in development is equally so.

» *What should caregivers and teachers know about the brain and how it influences development?*

» *Which is more important for the developing brain – nature or nurture?*

Development depends on the interaction between nature and nurture, often called heredity and environment. Years ago, it was thought that only genes contributed to brain development, but today scientists say both factors are critical to healthy brain development. For instance, when we talk about domestic violence or stress, especially during the second trimester when the baby's brain is developing and important nerve connections are forming, nurture is vital, but as the couple from Britain demonstrated, better late than never.

Stimulating parental engagement with children and the environment in which they live is vital for child development (Clare, 2012). Lack of stimulation through play, sounds and touch will inhibit physical movement or motor skills (Becket and Taylor, 2010, pp 148–9). Abilities for physical movement change through childhood from the largely involuntary movement patterns of the young infant to the highly skilled voluntary movements characteristic of later childhood and adolescence. In normal circumstances the speed of motor development is rapid in early life and, like physical growth, motor development shows predictable patterns of top-to-bottom and centre-to-extremities development, with movements at the head and in the more central areas coming under control before those of the lower part of the body or the hands and feet. The infant's movement develops in stages from creeping on all fours to standing while holding on to something and then standing unaided.

Physical development and a healthy brain, however, cannot happen if the child does not have an interactive relationship with the outside world. Yon was neglected and was denied this interactive relationship and so, quite simply, his brain did not grow. Yon did not receive sensory stimulation from the carers in the Romanian orphanage, there was no one there with the time to play with him, read or cuddle him. The ability of an infant's brain to change according to stimulation is known as plasticity, and from this children gain the essential psychological strengths of attachment, resilience and empathy. As we have seen with Yon, a lack of physical and emotional care-giving can lead to brain damage, but can also lead to physical consequences, as with our next case study.

CASE STUDY

Terry

Psychosocial dwarfism is a rare condition. The symptoms include decreased growth hormone and somatomedin secretion, very short stature, weight that is inappropriate for the height and an immature skeletal age. This disease is a progressive one, and as long as the child is left in the stressing environment, his or her cognitive abilities continue to degenerate. Though rare in the population at large, it is a result of children being kept in abusive, confined conditions for extended lengths of time. It can cause the body to completely stop growing but is generally considered to be temporary; regular growth will resume when the source of stress is removed. Terry was five when I first met him at his home and clearly small in stature. The home was sterile and his parents were lacking in emotional warmth. We removed Terry from his home and placed him with warm, cuddling foster carers. Within three months he was growing and continued to do so.

Critical reflection

As practitioners we sometimes have to look to unusual and rare causes of a child's limited development. How can we keep this in mind in our practice?

In the cases of Terry and Yon we can see how brain and body are interconnected and how the development of the brain is key to how we as human beings are able to grow and develop successfully or not. A key part of this development, especially in the early years, is motor skills.

Critical reflection

At the time of writing, early years education, particularly nursery care, is increasingly being expected to introduce more formal methods of teaching and assessment. This goes against what many of us see as the purpose of nursery education, for instance free play or forest school activity.

» *How do you feel about these tensions in early years education?*

Physical well-being

In 2008 Frank Furedi published the second edition of his book *Paranoid Parenting* in which he argues that children have become an obsession of policymakers, the media and the child-protection industry, who appear to relish lecturing parents on how to parent. I was lucky I became a parent before the media and government became so involved. I parented from what we had picked up, through common sense and trial and error and our sons have turned out just fine. I was not governed by political mantra, consumerism or expert views, but by common sense and my own learning as I went along. No one warned me that baby boys pee in your face when changing their nappy or about the emotions you experience when a two-year-old has a screaming tantrum in the supermarket and everyone looks at you as if you are a monster. The quasi experts that dictate good parenting and appropriate child growth attempt to tell us what is 'right' and to some extent feed into the Foucaultian idea of state control, yet at the same time create paranoid parents. Previously I have talked about health-compromising behaviours such as drug or alcohol misuse, but there are other lifestyle choices that parents make that also impact upon the physical welfare of the child. Breastfeeding v formula feeding is one such controversy.

It is not uncommon that nursing mothers receive negative comments from their relatives, friends, strangers and practitioners about how they feed their baby. Mothers study the often contradictory arguments in support of breastfeeding and against formula feeding. Both sides argue forcibly for what they think is right, but each mother is different and needs to be able to make informed decisions about herself and her baby. Some women and practitioners, feeling very emphatic about breastfeeding, become so-called breastfeeding activists, or 'lactivists', promoting breastfeeding in various ways, forgetting there are some sound medical reasons for bottle feeding, for example if the mother needs a medication that would be very harmful to the baby. Some women also have hypoplastic (underdeveloped) breasts and their breasts don't have enough milk-making tissue. In these cases, or when the mother has simply made the choice to bottle feed, the mother needs support not condemnation, but sometimes the enthusiastic lactivists come on too strongly and push their views too forcibly, leaving some mothers desponded and with a sense of failure.

CASE STUDY

Melanie and Charlotte

Melanie was a 20-year-old new mum without the immediate support of family. She was desperate to do what was right by her new daughter Charlotte. Melanie wanted to be a good parent. She attended all the classes, read the books, watched the programmes and listened to the advice the professionals gave her. In particular she took note of what the midwife and health visitor had said about how breastfeeding was best for the baby. She had deliberately not taken the pack left her by the formula representative in the maternity unit. She went home alone and did her best to breastfeed. The health visitor did not get to visit for six days and when she did she found Melanie in a distressed state and Charlotte weighing significantly less than she had done at birth. Charlotte was taken to hospital and social services were called.

The social worker allocated the case was experienced and quickly assessed what had happened. Charlotte was seen as a child in need and not one needing protection. With help and support Melanie switched to formula feeding and both mother and daughter were soon reunited at home.

Critical reflection

»   *Do you know if you were breastfed? Has it made a difference to you?*

»   *How do you react when you see a woman breastfeeding in a public place?*

Once the decision about breast or bottle feeding is made, the parent will be faced with further decisions about eating habits, physical activity, rest and sleep. Some children demonstrate patterns of behaviour (eg eating disorders) that may jeopardise their physical well-being. Parents are told that they need to provide their child with a healthy and balanced diet to ensure physical growth and well-being. We are told that by avoiding too much sugar, fat and additives, we will decrease the likelihood of later health-related problems such as obesity. We know that a balanced diet has a direct impact on physical growth and mental development. The government introduced the 'five a day' campaign encouraging parents to make sure that children are getting five portions of fruit or vegetables each day.

The public health debate

The 'what is right?' debate is nowhere more apparent than in relation to diet, food fads and allergies and, particularly in the early years, the pressure to breastfeed. The 'five a day' campaign was but one of a raft of initiatives sponsored by the government, from improving the quality of school meals (led by television chef Jamie Oliver) to campaigns to persuade parents to get children away from screens and into physical activities and sports. Indeed as the second half of the twentieth century came to an end the government involved itself more and more in suggesting to parents the best diet and healthy activities for their children. This approach was based on health education rather than prevention and reflected the general move in health policy. The success of the inoculation and then vaccine programme during the middle part of the twentieth century had eradicated many serious diseases such as polio and smallpox, free school meals had improved diet, improving healthcare had led to a healthier population and improved maternity care had children being offered a diagnosis and treatment. The vaccination programme is set out below.

Age	Vaccine
2 months	5-in-1 (DtaP/IPV/Hib) vaccine. This single vaccine protects the child against five separate diseases: diphtheria, tetanus, pertussis (whooping cough), polio and Haemophilus influenzae type b (Hib, a bacterial infection that can cause severe pneumonia or meningitis in young children). Also Pneumococcal (PCV) vaccine Rotavirus vaccine

Age	Vaccine
3 months	5-in-1 (DTaP/IPV/Hib) vaccine, second dose Also Meningitis C Rotavirus vaccine, second dose
4 months	5-in-1 (DTaP/IPV/Hib) vaccine, third dose Also Pneumococcal (PCV) vaccine, second dose
12/13 months	Hib/Men C booster, given as a single jab containing meningitis C (second dose) and Hib (fourth dose) Measles, mumps and rubella (MMR) vaccine, given as a single jab Pneumococcal (PCV) vaccine, third dose
3 years and 4 months	Measles, mumps and rubella (MMR) vaccine, second dose 4-in-1 (DTaP/IPV) pre-school booster, given as a single jab containing vaccines against diphtheria, tetanus, whooping cough (pertussis) and polio

As suggested when talking about birth choices it was once the case that people simply did what medical and nursing professionals said and did not question or look for alternatives. By the time we reached the 1990s, however, the public quite rightly were willing to question what was being told to them and to actively seek information on the internet and consider alternatives. This was true in all aspects of life, but in particular with medicine.

The MMR vacine is an immunisation vaccine against measles, mumps and rubella and is a mixture of live viruses of the three diseases. The MMR vaccine is generally administered to children around the age of one year, with a second dose before they start school. A second dose is administered to provide immunity to those who did not gain it after the first. Prior to the MMR vaccination being introduced in 1988, each year approximately half a million children in the UK caught measles with some 100 children dying from it or subsequent complications.

In the UK, the MMR vaccine was the subject of controversy after publication of academic papers in 2001 and 2002 reporting a small study of children who had bowel symptoms along with autism or other disorders, including cases where onset was believed by the parents to be soon after administration of the MMR vaccine. In 2010, Wakefield's research was found by the General Medical Council to have been *dishonest*, and *The Lancet* fully retracted the original paper (Anderberg et al, 2011). Many parents had decided against allowing their child to be given the vaccine while the controversy raged and it led to immunisation rates falling. Here was an example of the public being given a choice through the dissemination of information, bogus or otherwise, and coming to the 'wrong' conclusions. The consequences of this became apparent at the beginning of 2013 when there was a serious measles epidemic in Wales because some parents had failed to take up the offer of the MMR vaccine when they had the chance to do so.

Critical reflection

Some primary schools in England have introduced a policy that refuses entry to children who have not had the MMR vaccine because of the risk.

» *As a parent or practitioner how would you feel if the nursery or reception class attached to your local school refused to accept children that had not had the MMR jab?*

Conclusion

Children the world over grow from birth in the same way and more or less to the same timetable. They gain family and cultural features that distinguish each individual from the next and each human grouping. The physical needs of children are reasonably obvious. Without food and shelter a child will suffer harm and may die. The political and economic conditions in Western economies enable the majority of parents to fulfil these needs. On the other hand the child's intangible, non-material moral, spiritual, psychological and social needs are generally acknowledged to be more difficult to fulfil, and are often neglected. Yet a child deprived of its non-material needs will also suffer enormously and develop physical, emotional and social deficits, as we have seen with Yon and Terry. A child needs a package of care that includes all the elements above and is delivered by loving parents or parent.

Summary

When talking about physical development it is impossible not to make links to the psychological. The two are fused together and demonstrate how they are dependent on each other if we are to achieve positive outcomes for the child. We examined the growth of the physical child from conception to five years old and considered how we can maintain the child's physical well-being. We have considered how the government, through public health policy, tries to determine how children's health and well-being should be managed for the greater good, but also how information can bring negative as well as positive results when used by parents to make decisions.

Critical reflection

When did you last observe a baby? Maybe you never have. Find one soon and observe it over as long a period as possible. You might try to get a place in a baby room in a nursery, persuade a relative to let you care for theirs or watch your own. Observe how they develop so quickly.

Taking it further

I would strongly encourage you to undertake research on neuroscience, a subject that is fast changing our understanding of how the brain and body work together. Consider reading:

Carter, R (2013) *The Brain Book*. London: Medimation.

Also consider:

Horwath, J (2010) *The Child's World*. London: Jessica Kingsley.

Page, J, Clare, A and Nutbrown, C (2013) *Working with Babies and Children: From Birth to Three*. London: SAGE.

Rabinow, P (ed.) (1984) *The Foucault Reader*. London: Penguin.

And for children:

Diamond, M and Scheibel, A (1985) *The Brain Colouring Book*. London: Harper Collins.

References

Anderberg, D, et al (2011) Anatomy of a Health Scare: Education, Income and the MMR Controversy in the UK. *Journal of Health Economics*, 30 (3): 515-630.

Becket, C and Taylor, H (2010) *Human Growth and Development*. London: SAGE.

Clare, A (2012) *Creating a Learning Environment for Babies and Toddlers*. London: SAGE.

Furedi, F (2008) *Paranoid Parenting*. London: Continuum.

Mukherji, P and Dryden, L (eds) (2014) *Foundations of Early Childhood*. London: SAGE.

Rabinow, P (ed) (1984) *The Foucault Reader*. London: Penguin.

Ridley, M (2003) *Nature via Nurture*. London: Harper.

3 The psychological child

Learning outcomes:

*   to identify current thinking and theory in relation to the psychological child;

*   to recognise key concepts, such as attachment, resilience and empathy;

*   to consider the 'moral' child;

*   to understand communication and language development;

*   to consider education in the early years.

Critical question

The brain and body are dependent on each other and between them they determine how a child will develop. Most children develop reasonably well, but those in hard-to-reach families struggle to develop to their full potential.

»   *What role does the early years practitioner have in improving life chances for children?*

Introduction

Adults quickly forget what it is like to be a child, to see the world from a child's point of view and to think like a child. We grow up and become adults. The idea of 'becoming' (Lee, 2005) underpins much theoretical writing on children and childhood, assuming that being a child is often all about becoming an adult. Such activities and concerns with regard to children are reflected in growing academic engagement with the meaning and value of childhood. Scholars have attended increasingly to children's lives and what threatens them as conditioned by changes in material conditions and ideological formations, and as depicted over the centuries in painting and iconography or in personal, religious, medical or legal texts. Indeed, for a long while we only saw the physical child, not seeing and certainly not understanding the inner child. This chapter will attempt to demonstrate that over the last hundred years or so our understanding of the inner child has developed. We have learned more about how the child develops psychologically, building up the multi-layered view we now have. Outside the boundaries of any single discipline, it has been argued that childhood is a distinctively modern construction that has been shaped significantly by, for example, psychological and therapeutic ideas.

The inner child and important theorists

The emergence of the discipline of psychology during the nineteenth century and early twentieth century brought new explorations of the capacities, desires, needs and vulnerabilities of children, and has had considerable impact on parenting and teaching since. This is the period when we see the development of the 'unconscious child' with Freud and the growth of interest in the psyche and the 'naturally developing child' model with Piaget. In time and even in much of our current thinking, Freud, Piaget and their disciples came to dominate child psychological development thinking.

Sigmund Freud (1856–1939)

Freud introduced the psychoanalytic method for treating mental disturbance, or to control behaviour that was deemed as abnormal or a threat to society. He was the first medically trained neurologist to decide to use purely psychological means to treat his patients. The aim of psychoanalysis was to alleviate painful states. In respect to the understanding and study of children, Freud's impact should not be underestimated. Since Freud, successive generations of psychoanalysts have extended the range of conditions that can be treated psychoanalytically, including the treatment of children and adolescents. The use of psychiatry remains a significant method of dealing with 'difficult' children, as we have seen during the latter part of the twentieth century with the diagnostic labelling of children with behaviour difficulties as having ADHD and so forth.

Freud's work was wide-ranging, but we can draw out certain aspects that are useful when observing children. Freud argued that, as children develop, they become fixated on different and specific objects through their stages of development. At first they enter the oral stage and become fixated on feeding from the nipple, and then the anal stage as demonstrated by the toddler's pleasure in evacuating his or her bowels. In the phallic stage the child becomes fixated on their genitals. In this third stage, Freud contended, male infants become fixated on the mother (Oedipus Complex) as a sexual object and girls become fixated on the father (Electra Complex). When observing children we can identify these basic three stages, but we have to question Freud's assertions about the sexual objectification of parents by their children (Becket and Taylor, 2010, pp 37–9).

Jean Piaget (1896–1980)

Piaget was a Swiss developmental psychologist best known for his epistemological studies with children and his theory of cognitive development. Piaget's theory places its emphasis on discontinuities in child development, arguing that children pass through the given stages of development as follows:

- the sensorimotor stage (0–2 years);
- the pre-operational stage (2–7 years);
- the concrete operational stage (7–11 years);
- the formal operational stage (11–16 years).

Piaget distinguished between development and learning, believing development to be a spontaneous whole, in contrast to the limited nature of learning. He did not understand the symbiotic relationship between the various elements that create the child. Piaget believed that there were four main factors in the development of one set of structures from another: maturation, experience, social transmission and equilibration. His theory is essentially constructivist, avoiding discussions about nature and nurture. One of the main themes is that of adaptation: individuals, like biological species, develop as a result of continuous adaptation to the environment.

Piaget is rightly criticised on a number of points. His timetable of development is too prescriptive, the model is based on Western thinking and he believed, like Freud, that young children were fundamentally egocentric, and therefore unable to adapt successfully to viewpoints other than their own. One implication of this is that, according to Piaget, infants and young children are not social beings in the way that adults are. For our purpose the major shortcoming of Piaget's theory is his unwillingness to fully consider the degree of interplay between different aspects of development: social and cognitive, social and linguistic, and of course language and thought, including imagination and fantasy. Such theoretical points of divergence represent the starting point for a comparison between Piaget and Lev Vygotsky.

Lev Vygotsky (1896–1934)

Although Vygotsky was a contemporary of Piaget, his work did not appear in the West until the 1960s. Born in 1896, Vygotsky was Russian, a teacher, psychologist and scientist with an interest in how children learn. When his work became available it had a great influence on Western psychology's views of child development, which had up until that point tended to take Piaget's view, with an emphasis on the importance of the child's own personal cognitive development and the model of the child as a 'lone scientist'. Vygotsky developed the Zone of Proximal Development (ZPD) around the child, arguing that any significant adult, such as a teacher, could have a positive influence on the child and help them to develop. A child without positive role models – remember Yon – could not develop as fast as a child with them.

Critical reflection

So we have a tension between Piaget's view that childhood is the road to travel to become an adult and the view that childhood is a time for experience in its own right. What is your view?

We can also see the debate between the passive child, simply developing through stages, and the active child, open to the influences around them.

» *Do you support Piaget or Vygotsky, or take from both?*

Jerome Bruner (1915–)

If you support Vygotsky then scaffolding theory is something you may identify with. It was first introduced in the late 1950s by Jerome Bruner, a cognitive psychologist. He used the term to describe young children's oral language acquisition and how, helped by their parents, carers and practitioners, when they first start learning to speak, young children are provided with informal instructional schemas within which their learning is facilitated. An example given by Bruner is when parents read bedtime stories to their children and there is interaction between adult and child. We can see how scaffolding comes from Lev Vygotsky's concept of an expert assisting a novice. As practitioners, when assessing and observing, we see how children with positive scaffolding – active and positive parental support – can do better than those without.

John Bowlby (1907–90)

As our understanding of the child grew, we began to see the importance of the relationship between parents and their children and how that relationship impacts on the child's development. This is how nurture influences nature. Perhaps the most important theory to arise has been attachment, a deep and enduring emotional bond that connects one person to another across time and space. It does not have to be reciprocal and one person may have an attachment with an individual that is not shared. Bowlby characterised his theory by identifying specific behaviours in children, such as seeking proximity with the attachment figure when upset or threatened. He argued that attachment behaviour in adults towards the child includes responding sensitively and appropriately to the child's needs. Such behaviour appears universal across cultures and attachment theory provides an explanation of how the parent–child relationship emerges and influences subsequent development.

Bowlby was a psychiatrist working with children and this experience led him to consider the importance of the child's relationship with their mother in terms of their social, emotional and cognitive development. Specifically, it shaped his belief about the link between early infant separation with the mother and later dysfunctional behaviour. He observed that children experienced intense distress when separated from their mothers and in his view this was the basis for long-term relationships. He saw attachment as something that was a lasting psychological connection, specifically between mother and child, and proposed that attachment provides safety and security for the infant. Bowlby argued that children come into the world biologically pre-programmed to form attachments with others, because this will help them to survive (Maynard and Powell, 2014, pp 93–5). The infant produces innate behaviours such as crying and smiling that stimulate innate care-giving responses from adults. The determinant of attachment is not food but care and responsiveness. According to attachment theory infants have a universal need to seek close proximity with their caregiver when under stress or threatened:

- Up to 3 months: indiscriminate attachments. The newborn is predisposed to attach to any human and responds equally to any caregiver.

- After 4 months: preference for certain people. Infants learn to distinguish between primary and secondary caregivers but accept care from anyone.

- After 7 months: special preference for a single attachment figure develops and the baby looks to particular people for security, comfort and protection. It shows fear of strangers and unhappiness when separated from a special person (separation anxiety).

- After 9 months: multiple attachments. The baby becomes increasingly independent and may have formed many attachments by 10 months, including those to its mother, father, grandparents, siblings and family friends.

The most important fact in forming attachments is not who feeds and changes the child but who plays and communicates with him or her. The primary carer, normally the mother, is the one with whom the link is most important. Bowlby suggested that a child would initially form only one primary attachment and that the attachment figure acted as a secure base for exploring the world. The attachment relationship acts as a prototype for all future social relationships, so disrupting it can have severe consequences.

This theory also suggests that there is a critical period for developing attachment (about 0–5 years). Bowlby believed that if an attachment was not developed during this period then the child would suffer developmental consequences, such as a lack of empathy, and would struggle to form attachments as they progressed through life. Bowlby was not aware of how the brain grows and as we have previously discussed we now know that a lack of attachment from birth may indeed reduce the growth of neurons and leave dead areas in the brain that will have an impact on emotional well-being. This is dramatically demonstrated when we look at a scan of a Romanian orphan's brain, such as with Yon. But we also know that with reasonably early intervention from loving, committed parents these need not be irreversible.

CASE STUDY

Amanda, Part 2

As Amanda grew through infancy Jenny and Simon came to realise the care demands a child with cystic fibrosis places on her carers and the pressure it brings to a relationship. Despite counselling and support from her wider family Jenny continued to struggle with the idea that she had 'given' the disorder to her daughter.

With the help of social services a nursery place was found for Amanda and regular respite care was introduced into the family's routine. Grandparents also began to take an increasing role in Amanda's care, but all this positive help only seemed to widen the emotional gap between Amanda and her mother. As one nursery worker wrote in her log: *It feels as though Amanda is more attached to me than to Jenny. I don't know what to do about this?*

Youngsters with chronic illness, serious injuries and physical disabilities often benefit from modifications in instruction, equipment and their physical environment. Ultimately, educators should strive to make experiences as normal as possible for these children.

Critical question

» *Can you identify attachment in the children you work with or come across?*

Critical reflection

Let us consider the nursery worker's concern and what we might call the dilemma of practitioner love. Early years practitioners, childcare social workers and primary school teachers in particular find themselves drawn towards certain children and have to make certain appropriate boundaries are in place. Having said this, it is important that practitioners are free and safe to provide children with professional love and to allow attachments to take place. Vygotsky, remember, argues that children need significant adults in their lives to draw the best out of them.

» *Can the practitioner love of workers be used to help build attachments between Amanda and her mother? And if so, how might this be done?*

While attachment is vitally important it is only one of the factors we should be looking for when assessing. It is also important to remember that attachment can have a negative impact as well as positive and can influence a child's understanding of right and wrong.

Moral development

When I was about six I killed a cabbage white butterfly with a croquet mallet. I still remember chasing it around my aunt's garden until I finally brought the mallet crashing down upon it. I remember feeling horrified, ashamed and guilty and carefully burying it as the tears rolled down my cheeks. I kept saying sorry. I was afraid of my aunt finding out, but I was also desperate to make amends. I knew what I had done was wrong. Speaking to other men I have discovered that many of us killed small creatures in our early years and felt similar emotions, whereas a small number, most of whom I spoke to while working in prisons, did not regret what they had done and eventually went on to kill much larger prey. So what was happening for me when I killed the hapless butterfly? Was I old enough to have moral boundaries? I certainly knew right from wrong and understood the implications of punishment. There was empathy and remorse. So where had these feelings come from?

Lawrence Kohlberg (1927–87)

Kohlberg was an American psychologist best known for his theory of the stages of moral development. He argued that there are six identifiable developmental moral stages, each more sophisticated at responding to moral dilemmas than its predecessor. Kohlberg (Rathus, 2007) followed the development of moral judgement far beyond the stages studied earlier by Piaget, who claimed that logic and morality develop through constructive levels of understanding. Expanding on Piaget's work, Kohlberg determined that the process of moral development was principally concerned with justice, and that it continued throughout the individual's lifetime as follows:

Level 1 (pre-conventional)

1.   Obedience and punishment orientation (How can I avoid punishment?)

2.   Self-interest orientation (What am I getting out of this?)

Level 2 (conventional)

3.   Interpersonal accord and conformity (Social norms) (Right and wrong)

4.   Authority and social-order maintaining orientation (Law and order morality)

Level 3 (post-conventional)

5.   Social contract orientation

6.   Universal ethical principles (Principled conscience)

The understanding gained in each stage is retained in later stages, but may be regarded by those in later stages as simplistic, lacking in sufficient attention to detail.

In respect to children in the early years we need to concentrate on the pre-conventional level of moral reasoning. This is common in children, although adults can also exhibit this level of reasoning. Children judge the morality of an action by its direct consequences. So when I killed the butterfly I was worried about my aunt finding out and punishing me. The pre-conventional level consists of the first and second stages of moral development, and is solely concerned with the self in an egocentric manner. A child with pre-conventional morality has not yet adopted or internalised society's conventions regarding what is right or wrong, but instead focuses largely on external consequences that certain actions may bring. In Stage one (obedience and punishment driven), individuals focus on the direct consequences of their actions on themselves.

Stage two (self-interest driven) argues the *What's in it for me?* position, in which right behaviour is defined by whatever the individual believes to be in their best interest, but understood in a narrow way which does not consider one's reputation or relationships to groups of people. Stage two reasoning shows a limited interest in the needs of others, but only to a point where it might further the individual's own interests. As a result, concern for others is not always based on loyalty or instinctive respect, but rather as a basis for negotiation – *I'll look after you if you look after me*. The lack of a social perspective at the pre-conventional level is quite different from the social contract (Stage five), as all actions have the purpose of serving the individual's own needs or interests.

Empathy

Empathy is an emotional capacity that develops during early childhood and is also an important component of positive social behaviour. To function successfully in society – to negotiate, form friendships and so forth – we need to have good empathising skills. Again, as with other emotions, the development of empathy depends on cognitive and language development. Children who cannot engage in abstract thinking or take someone else's perspective are typically unlikely to respond with empathy; for instance, someone suffering from Asperger's syndrome (Ridley, 2003, p 62).

Reflective empathy is the ability to take another person's perspective in order to understand what they're feeling. Children with reflective empathy can understand the causes, effects and behavioural cues characteristic of various emotions in a sophisticated way. As a result, they start to understand that certain emotional cues can suggest what another person is feeling. Cues may include another person's facial expressions, spoken thoughts or behaviours such as laughing or crying. Young children may also be able to predict, based on their prior learning, someone's emotional response from the context of the event, such as anticipating that someone who accidentally cuts his or her finger will be hurting. This is one of the reasons why it is important to leave the nettles in the playground, for unless children experience hurt themselves they will not comprehend it in others. As children first develop reflective empathy, the feelings can seem overwhelming because they do not know how to comfort or help the other person. Children may start experiencing the situation as if it were actually happening to them and become distressed. So if Yon had continued to grow up in the orphanage and see another child hurt itself he would probably not have shown any empathy, but a child with developing empathy might become so upset or scared imagining the injured child's feelings that he/she might start crying too. However, as children continue to develop cognitively, they learn strategies for comforting or helping other people.

Communication and language

It always annoys me when students or practitioners comment verbally, in an observation or in a report, that because a baby does not speak you cannot tell what it is feeling or thinking. While talking is important, we all begin to communicate from the moment we are born. A cry and a smile are both communications, but it is true that language is the primary means by which humans communicate with each other. Language is a cultural tool which provides the means for members of a group to retain their shared identity and to relate to each other (Maynard and Powell, 2014, pp 54–5) to avoid misunderstandings, to teach, to explain themselves, to build relationships, to articulate love and where necessary to warn others about danger. Indeed, it might be argued that language came from the need to warn others (*There is a bear behind you*) or to negotiate away from violent situations (*It's your turn to clean the cave*). While Piaget places little emphasis on language, Vygotsky sees it as central to building the learning relationship within the ZPD (Becket and Taylor, 2010, p 72). Through the process of language learning, as previously touched upon in relation to Bruner and scaffolding theory, parents, education, media and peer groups help to socialise children into socially and culturally appropriate ways of behaving, speaking and thinking.

CASE STUDY

Monique and Ivan

Monique was a young mum of nineteen married to a serving soldier away on active service in Afghanistan. Monique and their two-year-old son Ivan lived in an army quarter on an estate with other young mums. There was a twice weekly mother and toddler group held at the garrison church hall run by the Army Welfare Service. The worker running the group had noticed that Monique tended to use negative language towards Ivan, criticising him when he did something 'wrong' and not praising him when he needed it. Since attending the group Ivan's behaviour had become disruptive and other mums had started to complain. The worker made a point of getting to know Monique and of not rushing into correcting her, especially not in front of the other mums. The worker arranged to visit Monique at home and from there began to work with her not only on the language she was using with Ivan, but also on providing support for Monique to help her manage her feelings of isolation, loneliness and inadequacy.

The worker demonstrated three essential skills of the early years practitioner:

* to observe and assess and not rush in;
* to relate theory to practice and understand the needs of the child;
* to take an holistic view, recognising that Monique had other needs.

Language acquisition

The process of learning a language for young children is built upon a variety of experiences and it begins from birth, with parents and caregivers involved with infants in communicative exchanges. These exchanges accompany activities shared by adults and infants, such as feeding and playing. During these activities, parents, caregivers and practitioners comment on the child's actions and often repeat and exaggerate their vocalisations – *You are such a good boy, Mummy is very proud of you!* – when a child successfully uses the potty. Such communicative exchanges between adults and infants function as a form of social interaction and reinforcement. The child will mimic the care-giving adult. Here we should remind ourselves that negative comments are as powerful as positive comments, and rather than building a child's confidence and self-esteem they can be damaging and abusive. Social interaction helps build attachment, enhances a child's interests in their environment and provides them with stimulation for language development.

There are a number of theories as to how children develop language, including the behaviourist that focuses on imitation, cognitive theory that comes with maturation, constructivist that sees language developing with use, and social-interactavist, supported by Vygotsky and Bruner, that argues that language comes with social contact (Mukherji and Dryden, 2014, p 323).

Critical reflection

Explore the theoretical models above by undertaking some practitioner research and decide which one you feel is the strongest. Or perhaps they all have a part to play?

In the chart below I have set out approximate vocalisation developments in relation to age that we can observe as the child develops their communication skills.

Approximate age	Observation
Babies	Crying is the earliest form of vocalisation. But after only a few weeks of experience with language, infants begin to vocalise in addition to crying, varying the sounds they make by cooing and gurgling. Parents should begin to recognise these sounds and associate them with different needs. This represents the linkage between communication and sound-making and signals the onset of language.
Four months plus	At this stage children should start to add consonant sounds and they begin to 'babble'. Infants are able to combine these consonant and vowel sounds into syllable-like sequences, such as 'mama'. It is essential that parents, caregivers and practitioners interact with babies, infants and young children through language. If they do not or if the child is isolated, then the child will struggle to develop language.
One year	By the beginning of the first year, children's first words will be emerging. At this stage children's productive vocabulary usually contains only simple words, and they will utter single words to represent the whole meaning of an entire sentence. They will often use a single word to identify something or somebody under different conditions (such as saying 'mama' when seeing their mother), to label objects linked to someone or something such as saying 'pussy' when they see the cat's bowl, or to express needs, eg saying 'potty'. In the initial stage of the first-word utterance, children produce words slowly but then quickly begin to gain new words and develop a reasonable vocabulary.
Two years	By now most children begin to combine words and to generate simple sentences. Children's first sentences are like a mobile phone text, often only containing the essential content words, such as verbs and nouns, but omitting the function words, such as articles, prepositions and pronouns. Although children's first sentences seem to be ungrammatical in adult terms, they can be very communicative and get directly to the point. They have a structure of their own. An example would be 'more apple'.

Approximate age	Observation
Three–four years	By the time children are 3 to 4 years of age, they have already acquired many important skills in language learning. They have a fairly large working vocabulary and an understanding of the function of words in referring to things and actions. They also have a command of basic conversational skills, such as talking about a variety of topics with different listeners. Nevertheless, language development, especially vocabulary growth and conversational skills, continues with interacting with others, for instance during meal times, at pre-school and during play. Feedback, as opposed to correction, by adults is an important part of this process. Children are well able to interpret what is being said and to make links to things they have seen and heard elsewhere.
Four–five years	By the time children enter the Reception class at primary school their oral language is very similar to that of adults, having acquired the basic syntactic, semantic and pragmatic elements of their native language. It is important that practitioners have some insight into the cultural background of the child in order to help the child adjust to the language environment of the classroom.

I have already sought to place emphasis on the importance of parental, and where appropriate practitioner, interaction with children. In respect to language acquisition it is absolutely vital. Listening and talking with caregivers from birth allows the child to steadily increase its understanding of language and to grow a vocabulary. The development of conversational skills also requires children's active interaction with other people. To communicate with others effectively – for instance, to demonstrate empathy – children need to learn how to negotiate, take turns and make relevant as well as intelligible contributions. Through interacting with other, more experienced language users, children modify and elaborate their sentences in response to requests for more information. In addition, young children learn to adjust their messages to their listeners' level of understanding, for instance to a younger sibling.

In summary, language learning is both a social and a developmental process. To acquire a language, children must interact with other, more competent language users as well as explore various aspects of the linguistic system. During the early years of language learning, children also create, test and revise their understanding regarding the use of language. Parents and early childhood practitioners should provide these young learners with developmentally appropriate language activities and offer opportunities for them to experiment with different aspects of language learning.

As our society becomes more diverse there will be the positive outcome of more children being bilingual, but at the same time there will be significant challenges for practitioners working with children. The children themselves may find themselves caught between two language/cultural worlds, not belonging to either (Maynard and Powell, 2014, pp 110–14).

Critical reflection

Observing and listening to children in conversation, either with their peers or cuddly toys, can give great insight into the development of language. Think about the age of the child and compare where they are developmentally with the theory.

»   *Do we apply our own expectations differently to our own children than to those we work with? If so, why?*

Early years education

Central government is currently concerned that a significant number of children struggle to find their feet in secondary school because primary schools have not provided them with the necessary basic skills in reading, writing and arithmetic. According to Department for Education figures published in 2013 only 61% of five-year-olds achieved the expected level in literacy and 66% in maths. So the question remains, how can we let any children pass through early years education without gaining the basics? To the government the answer appears simple: test and rank the children; inspect the nurseries and schools and if they are not meeting the required standards take the setting into special measures, especially if too many children are failing the tests. Some schools are not good enough and need prodding, but most of the reasons why children do not learn are caused by influences beyond a school's reach.

While we can highlight issues such as pupils not speaking English (for instance, there are over 70 languages spoken in Hampshire schools) and some children only arrive a year before their final test, home issues are especially significant. We have already talked about the importance of parents and carers working with children to develop language skills and so forth and where there is a lack of parental support, a chaotic home life or poor attendance problems are inevitably exacerbated. As some social conditions worsen, as the poor get poorer and more insecure, and as some children go hungry, schools are a great place of safety and calm. But they need to offer wrap-around services, from free breakfasts to after-school clubs, with community services inside the school. Some children who fail to learn are from the most chaotic, disadvantaged families, and have already had limited school experience. The amount of help available to families on the edge through depression, mental illness, cultural exclusion and addiction is limited, unless they reach a stage of abuse where a child may become the subject of a child protection investigation. The quality of nursery teaching is even more critical when considering disadvantaged families and the need to give a child the chance to rise above their negative experience. By focusing on academic achievement we run the risk of losing these children forever.

In Denmark children do not go to school until they are six, spending the previous years in kindergarten. Visiting Denmark on a regular basis to teach in one of the Copenhagen universities I had the chance to take English social care students to one of the kindergartens. Let me take you there now. Entering through the front gate we walk along a path that bisects the garden. There are nettles and blackberry bushes as well as flowers and a large lawn. Inside we discover a three-story building full of happy, laughing children. There are lighted candles, real knives for cooking and no stair gates. This is an environment in which children could learn about risk and how to manage it, and not one suffocated by health and safety concerns. By comparison with those in Denmark, English classrooms tend to be well resourced but cramped, and complex layouts add to their relative inflexibility.

Much more importance is attached in Denmark to the way early years children develop as people, rather than what they should know and be able to do. Although literacy and numeracy and other areas of learning are important in the Danish system, personal and social development, learning to learn, developing self-control and preparation for school are given a high priority. Much more is expected of English early years children in reading, writing and mathematics and English children are tested and labelled on their ability, something you do not find in Nordic systems. While it is true that in these specific areas of academic learning that the achievement of early years children in English schools is generally in advance of their counterparts in Denmark, we have to ask ourselves, what do we want from early years education? Do we want well-rounded children socially able and keen to learn or children that will pass exams? Even intensive academic education will not enable the disadvantaged or those children without academic ability. The danger is that the government is taking us down a cul-de-sac from which we will struggle to reverse and many children will be ultimately excluded from society. Even when Danish children go to school at six or seven, learning tasks in lessons have a clear social perspective while in England they have an emphasis on knowledge and skills. In Denmark, for instance, the emphasis is on acquiring positive attitudes to learning and an awareness of the feelings and needs of classmates and other people.

CASE STUDY

Yon, Part 2

Yon, you will remember from Chapter 2, was born in Bucharest and after spending a traumatic period in a Romanian nursery was adopted by a British couple from Portsmouth. They brought him back, provided him with physical and emotional affection in order to try to connect the missing links and achieved a great deal. Penny, his adoptive mother, remained at home to care for him, but when he reached two she decided it would be good for him to attend a nursery and for her to find a part-time job. Fortunately, there was a nursery with a pedagogic approach nearby in which free play and outside activity were a very important element.

Critical question

» *How important is it for a nursery to have an outside space? Why?*

Conclusion

In this chapter we have looked at the development of the psychological child, including the development of language and the role of education. We have considered the various factors and how these link and intertwine together to form the intricacies of the individual psyche. The importance of positive early psychological development cannot be underestimated in relation to the ongoing healthy growth of the child. The first 18 months are key to how the child, adolescent and adult will be.

Summary

In this chapter we have examined the development of the child's cognitive and psychological ability, recognising that these developments are as important as the physical. Indeed we have explored how the two are in fact dependent upon each other and that parents and carers have a vital role to play, for instance in relation to the ability to attach, to empathise and consider how the young child begins to develop a moral awareness.

Critical reflection

A child's physical development is reasonably easy to observe, but psychological and emotional development is more difficult.

» *How can we as practitioners gather evidence about these things when working with children in the early years?*

Taking it further

Take the opportunity to research and read about international systems of care and education, for instance in Scandinavia. See, for example:

Forsberg, H and Kroger, T (2001) *Social Work and Child Welfare Politics: Through Nordic Lenses*. Bristol: Polity Press.

See also:

Cree, V (2000) *Sociology for Social Workers and Probation Officers*. London: Routledge.

Daniel, B, Wassell, S and Gilligan, R (2010) *Child Development for Child Care and Protection Workers*. London: Jessica Kingsley.

James, A, Jenks, C and Prout, A (1998) *Theorizing Childhood*. Cambridge: Polity.

Jenks, C (2001) *Childhood*. London: Routledge.

Lindon, J (2012) *Understanding Child Development*. London: Hodder Education.

Page, J, Clare, A and Nutbrown, C (2013) *Working with Babies and Children*. London: SAGE.

References

Becket, C and Taylor, H (2010) *Human Growth and Development*. London: SAGE.

Lee, N (2005) *Childhood and Society*. Maidenhead: Open University Press.

Maynard, T and Powell, S (2014) *Early Childhood Studies*. London: SAGE.

Mukherji, P and Dryden, L (eds) (2014) *Foundations of Early Childhood*. London: SAGE.

Rathus, S (2007) *Childhood: Voyages in Development*. London: Wadsworth.

Ridley, M (2003) *Nature via Nurture: Genes, Experience and What Makes Us Human*. London: Harper.

4 The social child

Learning outcomes:

*   to identify external influences that shape the development of a young child and in so doing lay down the foundations for the adolescent and adult;

*   to explore the issues that inform our understanding of childhood;

*   to consider the place of childhood in our times;

*   to consider theory, in particular socialisation;

*   to consider how play is a vital means through which children learn social skills;

*   to examine the role of parents, peer groups and other social influences.

Critical question

»   *How do we protect childhood?*

Introduction

In this chapter I am going to examine the social child from two different directions, from the perspective of how the child becomes social and how society views the child. These views are connected and one feeds the other. I am also going to say something about modern childhood and how experiences during the early years lay down the foundations for later life.

We can say that children are all alike in that they are members of the same species and share the same biological and physiological characteristics, walk upright, have the potential for speech and so on. In this species sense, we can reasonably speak of the biological child who is like all other children. Physically, we know from forensic archaeology and anthropology, the physiological structure of the child has not changed very much at all. With this baseline we can move on to say that every child has key influences in its life that will be shared with others, but these make the individual child different from the next. We recognise that each child has a unique genetic endowment. According to Ridley (2003) genes are involved in every aspect of human behaviour. The precise way they are involved depends on complex feedback between the genes and the nurturing the child is given from conception. This does not mean that the environment overcomes genetics – nature versus nurture – but rather that the environment and nurture operate by influencing patterns of gene activity. As we discover how genes get turned on and off, how sensitive the key segments of DNA, called 'promoters', are to a host of influences, we see that the pattern of genetic activity comes to incorporate a record of environmental effects: nature via nurture. Nurturing is directed by two key influences. Firstly, it is true that only subgroups of children share the same language, culture and physical environment. When considering children who are like some other children in this cultural sense, we can speak of the social child. Secondly, each child will have different experiences in the particular circumstances of his or her upbringing. When we speak of children in this unique, individual sense, we might also speak of the social child.

Before examining the present I want to go back some years, to the end of the Middle Ages, when the main task for children was to survive to the age of six or seven, after which they disappeared into the world of adults. There was no social awareness of childhood – that is, of children as a separate social group. Childhood was not reflected in the home, children simply did not exist, or were regarded as their father's private property. Before the sixteenth century the legal view of the child was almost one of default in that the child itself was not a legal entity, only becoming so in terms of the father's property. Legal involvement at this time was mainly limited to issues of inheritance, in which the child was literally part of the property to be inherited. Legally the age of maturity in the sixteenth century was defined as *from the anniversary of the tenth birthday*; by the seventeenth century the age of maturity had risen to 12. The change in age at which childhood was at an end and adulthood began was not based on any biological or psychological assessment of the child's development, but more from the social constructions of the day. Henry de Bracton, a leading medieval English jurist and author, identified that: *In times past, girls and boys had soon attained the age [majority]: life was rude and there was not much to learn* (de Bracton, c.1260, cited in Humphries and Gully, 1999, p 4). He argued that prolonging the protection of infancy during the medieval period resulted not from any understanding of childhood, but rather for the poor a need to get the child out to work, and for the elite from the very practical introduction of heavy armour. The sons of the social elite could only be regarded as 'full age' when strong enough to bare armour and to fight as knights. The experience of children from the labouring poor was also linked to physical strength, but was different to that of the social elite, with the age of maturity younger and connected to the child's ability to labour with the family. The child was expected to work alongside their parents or otherwise to contribute to the family income as soon as physically able. This removed them at an early age from the child's world, a world that was not acknowledged in Western culture until the eighteenth century, when Rousseau characterised it as follows: *nature wants children to be children before they are men. If we deliberately pervert this order, we shall get premature fruits which are neither ripe nor well-flavoured, and which soon decay* (Jenks, 2005, p 3).

In Western society the child no longer has to be productive at the earliest opportunity and our children are not expected to fight in war. In both respects children born into Western society are fortunate compared to many growing up in the developing world where survival and war are often ways of life and children are expected to play an active part in both. We have developed laws for the protection of children, for social control and for compulsory education, and the consequences of this new attitude towards childhood is that children are excluded from the world of work and are placed into a waiting room, known as schools. Children have shifted from being the property solely of the parents to also being the property of the state, because the state is now involved more and more in the name of protecting children, and this intervention produces a tension not only between parents and the state, but also for children and young people. Childhood is the most intensively governed sector of personal existence as the modern child has become the focus of innumerable projects that purport to safeguard it from physical, sexual and moral danger, to ensure its 'normal' development.

During the nineteenth century we refined our version of childhood. We needed to get small fingers away from industry and we recognised their intelligence. So we placed them in education, and childhood developed as a kind of independent category, but not one in which they had the freedom to speak freely. Because even as the reforming twentieth century progressed, the *adultism* (Cree, 2000, p 57) in society meant that we still tended to see children and childhood through the eyes of adults. In history, where children are not seen by adults they do not exist. This is similar to the position of women prior to feminist sociology. *Childhood has been defined in opposition to adulthood. Growing up is often taken to be a process in which something (a child) becomes its opposite (an adult), a process in which the boundary between becoming and being is crossed* (Lee, 2005, p 8).

Critical reflection

In today's society there appears to be a great deal of pressure for children to grow up as quickly as possible. Even in the early years there is pressure to dress and behave like small adults, potentially undermining childhood.

» *Is this process now inevitable?*

Early years and social development

Sometimes I hear students and even professionals take lightly the idea that babies are social when we know that from the earliest moment babies begin to react to social contact. Contact with the mother is generally the first step in developing the social child. The baby learns the importance of physical and gradually emotional contact and these begin to feed the cognitive awareness that contact with other humans is good and rewarding. As the child grows other adults and children start to enter its world and influence the developing social child. Understanding and skills start to take shape, especially through play, and these are built upon until the young child is able to function independently of the primary carer. As I have already said, I was an only child and it is interesting to compare the differences between the social development I experienced with that of a child with immediate siblings. The differences are subtle but telling. With an only child the inner world may be more defined and the sense of self as one may be stronger. This can lead to a strong sense of independence, but a lack of developed social skills and even shyness that in some can be debilitating through later life.

Critical reflection

Think back to when you were a child. Were you an only child or one of a pair or more? How do you think your social development was affected?

Positive social development is key to us as individuals finding our place in our community and the wider society. It enables us to be a part of the world and to appreciate others.

CASE STUDY

Mandy and Peter – both aged 4

Mandy and Peter were playing in the paddling pool in the garden of the nursery. The other children had moved on to play in the sand pit. Peter was especially taken with a string of plastic green ducks that he was pulling enthusiastically through the water. He was making whooshing noises as he did so. So absorbed was he that he lost his footing and slipped headlong into the water. Shaking himself he managed to sit up, his face contorted and he appeared ready to cry, but then Mandy was at his side and her small hand was on his shoulder. He looked up into her face and both children began to laugh.

Critical reflection

In the case of Mandy and Peter we can see how a number of strands of psychological development have come together to influence their actions. We have empathy and emotional warmth from Mandy and resilience and self-responsibility from Peter. In both of them we can observe the development of social skills and a sense of humour.

» *As practitioners, what can we do to help children develop social skills?*

Socialisation

I am a great fan of Michel Foucault and find resonance with my own thinking in his views that society is geared to creating docile bodies, beings that generally follow the rules. *The classical age discovered the body as an object and target of power. It is easy enough to find signs of the attention then paid to the body – to the body that is manipulated, shaped, trained, which obeys, responds, becomes skilful and increases its forces* (Rabinow, 1995, p 136). Body shape is in itself a debate to be had, but for now let us remain with social docility, acceptance or what one might call socialisation. We get up, go to work, pay taxes, break a few laws, go home, watch television and so forth. There is little real rebellion. We are good citizens and this is what society sets out to do to children. Society is structured and made up of rules, regulations, values and beliefs. Authority maintains order and can be defined as legitimate power. It is an overall power, often having legal backing, which is accepted by most of us. Within society, institutions such as the family and schools have their own functions; child rearing is important to the maintenance of society. Children will glean many of their fundamental views from their parents about their own self, about their culture and about their potential. Poor role modelling may have a long-term impact upon their self-esteem and ability to achieve (Pugh and Duffy, 2014, pp 185–92).

There are many groups within society and they generally co-operate harmoniously. This is mainly due to value consensus, which is a widespread agreement about basic values, promoting co-operation in society. On the one hand this process begins in the early years with the pressure to feed, clothe and educate the child in a certain way. In response the child will develop through a number of stages (Wall, 2006, pp 80–3; Erikson, see section below in this chapter). Children can, however, set unique challenges to the society in which they are growing and it is my view that this is healthy and should be accepted and even encouraged, but there are limits; limits that should be set by authoritative parenting leading to a balanced approach between care and control.

Society demands certain things from its members, never more than in the case of children, and we try to modify their behaviour from birth to meet these demands. These modifying forces might be seen as a benefit to both individuals and society. In respect to children this has traditionally included obedience to adults and the view that stability and social order are vital for the survival of society. This follows the view of consensus theory that a particular political or economic system is a fair system, and that social change should take place within the social institutions provided by it, such as through democratic process. Consensus theory contrasts sharply with conflict theory, which holds that the key to society is conflict rather than harmony, arguing that stability is an illusion and social control is the source of unrest within society. Power, therefore, is considered to be the ability to control others – parents over children, men over women – and the theory focuses on the unequal distribution of power in society. Deviance can therefore be seen as a positive, inspiring creativity and social change. Adults tend not to see things this way and operational definitions of desirable skills and outcomes are likely to be highly adult-centred, and might neglect the child's own objectives. Children and young people are rebelling against this, finding a voice. On a recent visit to teach in Copenhagen I visited Christiania, the 'free' community over the river from the centre of the city where art and creativity thrives alongside the open selling of illegal substances. Here young people (and the not so young) are free to exist as they want and, in my opinion, it works. It follows that peer definition and assessment of social competence might be equally or more valid than adult assessment.

Critical question

» *Could we use peer assessment in the early years?*

With these dramatic changes in the nature of childhood and the knowingness of children can we still use the traditional theories to examine the social child? So, for instance, are the previously mentioned stages of moral development defined by Kohlberg still applicable, and is Erikson still relevant?

Erik Erikson 1902–94

A German-born American developmental psychologist, Erikson is best known for his theory on psychosocial development. He was the first to use the phrase 'identity crisis', and surely this can be used in relation to many children and young people in our society today? Erikson offers a developmental schema that remains central to much social and educational orthodoxy (see table below). According to Erikson, the socialisation process consists of eight phases (Beckett and Taylor, 2010). Erikson believed that every child experiences a series of psychosocial crises or identity crises. These stages are conceived in an architectural sense: the satisfactory resolution of each crisis is necessary if the child is to manage the next and subsequent ones satisfactorily. The first four stages can still be applied to children of this generation, as in attachment theory the early years remain predictable and protected from the new normal, but what about the later stages? Do children and young people still experience identity and intimacy and as we once did?

Intimacy is certainly open to question with the arrival of sexual grazing when the act becomes more important than the relationship. Today even the most well-adjusted of adolescents in our society experiences significant identity confusion: most boys and probably most girls experiment with minor delinquency and rebellion. There is little if any certainty for a child to hang on to. Young people are often paralysed by feelings of inadequacy when they judge themselves against social and adult expectations. The foundations for these uncertainties are laid down in the early years often as not by the uncertainty of parents and practitioners as to when to talk to children about gender, sexuality and so forth. As our society becomes more diverse, young minds will inevitably ask more questions and we have to be ready with the answers, however uncomfortable that may make us feel.

1	Aged one Learning basic trust v basic mistrust	Chronologically, this is the period of infancy through the first one or two years of life. The child, nurtured and loved, develops trust and security and a basic optimism. Badly handled, he becomes insecure and mistrustful. This can be linked to the development of attachment.
2	Aged two–three Learning autonomy v shame	The second psychosocial crisis occurs during early childhood, probably between about 18 months and three years of age. The 'well-parented' child emerges from this stage sure of herself and proud rather than ashamed. The child should be gaining some level of independence from caregivers.
3	Aged four–five Learning initiative v guilt	During this stage, the healthily developing child learns, through play (including fantasy) and social activities, to co-operate with others and widen her understanding of people and the environment. Here we can see the development of moral boundaries and empathy. The child that is emotionally neglected will be less sure of herself and will demonstrate a restricted connection with the world.

4	Aged six–eleven Industry v inferiority	The fourth psychosocial crisis is handled, for better or worse, during what Erikson calls the 'school age', presumably up to and possibly including the very early years of secondary school. Here the child learns to master the more formal skills of life. These will include relating with peers according to social rules, progressing from free play to structured play that may demand formal teamwork and mastering academic study.
5	Teenage years Learning identity v identity diffusion	Erikson argues that during the fifth psychosocial crisis the child, now an adolescent, can answer satisfactorily and happily the question of *Who am I?*
6	Young adulthood Learning intimacy v isolation	Upon reaching this stage the division between Erikson and reality is growing wide. According to him the young adult, for the first time, can experience true intimacy – the sort of intimacy that makes possible a good marriage or a genuine and enduring friendship.
7	Middle adulthood Learning generativity v self-absorption	In adulthood, the psychosocial crisis demands generativity, both in the sense of marriage and parenthood, and in the sense of working productively and creatively.
8	Late adulthood Integrity v despair	Here the mature adult develops the peak of adjustment; integrity. He trusts and is independent. He works hard, has found a well-defined role in life, and has developed a self-concept with which he is happy. If one or more of the earlier psychosocial crises have not been resolved, he may view himself and his life with despair.

Compiled and interpreted from a number of sources including Becket and Taylor (2010), Mukherji and Dryden (2014) and Rathus (2007).

Critical questions

»   *Consider Erikson's typology set out above and ask yourself if it can still be applied to the children you know and work with.*

»   *Are children growing up much quicker nowadays?*

The conflicted child

We might argue that this generation's children are in conflict on a number of fronts. The voice of the child is there to be heard and we as adults struggle to hear and or accept what it is saying. They have been through a gender revolution, which means that when they enter the education system or school they know that, whether they are a boy or girl, they should have the same opportunities in life, but personal sexual opportunities and pressures distort gender issues leaving many children confused and often abused. While nearly everyone these days has the opportunity to enter education, economic reality has taken it away. Many children are cash rich with a myriad of products that meet their consumer preferences, but the peer pressures to have the 'in' things or fit a particular body image has led to violence, bullying and mental health difficulties for some. What about technology and globalisation? If you ask children and young people today they have quite an overview of what the world is, but are not interested in politics. Music, gaming and fashion may be the things influencing the youngsters these days. The IT revolution is here. They are networked children, but despite all this play remains a vital ingredient in the lives of children, especially in the early years (Maynard and Powell, 2014, Chapter 5).

Play

Understanding the importance of play to children and being able to help children to play are key roles for parents and practitioners. Play is not simply fun, although it should always be fun, it is the medium through which children develop physically, psychologically, emotionally and socially. As we saw above with Mandy and Peter, through playing together they began to understand social skills and how to relate to others.

To some there may appear to be a tension between play and education. Play may be seen as unproductive in educational terms, but it is essential in facilitating learning. Communication and language development come through play as do the skills to problem solve and deal with conflict. Two children want the same toy and to begin with they may tussle over it, pulling and shoving, but as their skills develop they will begin to negotiate, using language to resolve the problem. They will learn to share and to build attachments, relationships and friendships.

Parents and practitioners need to be willing and able to plan playful activities when appropriate, but also to encourage free play when children's imaginations take over and a square of chairs become a castle or imaginary friends arrive for a picnic. Adults working with children must be willing to get down and dirty and fully engage with the playful activity or know when to step back and let the child have her own way.

We have to move with the fast-moving times and because the nursery is invaded by the fashion industry, the multimedia industry, remote controls and mobile phones we need to be ready to respond and make use of new technology to engage with children.

Critical reflection

» *Consider your own childhood and upbringing. How much have things changed since you became an adult?*

» *Do you remember playing? Did you have imaginary friends?*

» *As a parent/practitioner, do you enjoy playing with children?*

Conclusion

At a time when society is so focused on issues of childhood – including new definitions of the family, the ubiquitous term 'family values', risk avoidance, the body and genetic developments – we must remind ourselves that childhood is fluid and determined by social scientists rather than reality. Many of the attitudes we now hold concerning children and their special importance was not so long ago inconceivable. The way society thinks of children is a reflection of the period in which they are living. Despite this interest there remain significant problems in definition and identification, with changing visions, the lack of clearly defined compartments, shifting moral attitudes and the illusory and elusive nature of the subject. Nowhere is this change more evident than in family relationships. During the twentieth century, as the family came to be based more often on bonds of affection rather than economics, the child, once at the periphery, began its spiral towards the centre of family and society, yet no sooner had this happened than the new 'traditional' family began to shape shift. Science, IVF, surrogacy and so forth have combined with emancipation and tolerance, to bring us families in many shapes and hues.

While we struggle to define and maintain the family the argument has recently been inverted to suggest that post-modernity sets the scene for the disappearance of childhood, as many of the boundaries around children fall victim to a general erosion of linear sequences and stable categorisations. Some take the view that we have already entered into a dark age for children and young people, but I am forced to disagree. While the conflicts they face are significant I firmly believe that the future is in good hands and our children will overcome and find positive routes into the future.

Summary

We can observe the physical growth of the child and to a large extent measure the psychological growth of that child, but how can we know if the child is developing socially and if that development is positive? Perhaps the most important thing is that children experience broad social contact with adults and other children. That through play they can learn, understand and develop the skills to become well-rounded human beings. In the previous chapter on the development of the psychological child I argued for a more social-orientated approach to education as they have in Denmark and I would reiterate that plea right here.

Critical reflection

» *Look at children you know and/or work with and imagine them ten and twenty years from now. To what extent does the way they are now influence what they will become?*

» *In a world where technology is a growing influence on our social lives, how can practitioners and parents get the balance right?*

Taking it further

Technology and social networking are with us to stay and are part of children's lives even in the early years. I thoroughly recommend the following:

Marsh, J (2014) 'Childhood in the Digital Age', in Maynard, T and Powell, S, *Early Childhood Studies*. London: SAGE, Chapter 5.

In this chapter I briefly touched upon play. The brevity of the section fails to reflect the importance of play and the fun practitioners can have playing with children, and I would encourage you to read further. In particular, I recommend the following:

Howard, J (2014) 'Play and Development in Early Childhood', in Maynard, T and Powell, S, *Early Childhood Studies*. London: SAGE, Chapter 9.

See also:

Daniel, B, Wassell, S and Gilligan, R (2010) *Child Development for Child Care and Protection Workers*. London: Jessica Kingsley.

Horwath, J (2010) *The Child's World*. London: Jessica Kingsley.

Lindon, J (2012) *Understanding Child Development 0–8 Years*. London: Hodder Education.

Page, J, Clare, A and Nutbrown, C (2013) *Working with Babies and Children*. London: SAGE.

References

Becket, C and Taylor, H (2010) *Human Growth and Development*. London: SAGE.

Cree, V (2000) *Sociology for Social Workers and Probation Officers*. London: Routledge.

Humphries, L and Gully, T (1999) *Child Protection for Hospital-Based Practitioners*. London: WHURR.

Jenks, C (2005) *Childhood* (2nd Ed). London: Routledge.

Lee, N (2005) *Childhood and Society*. Maidenhead: Open University Press.

Maynard, T and Powell, S (2014) *Early Childhood Studies*. London: SAGE.

Mukherji, P and Dryden, L (eds) (2014) *Foundations of Early Childhood*. London: SAGE.

Pugh, G and Duffy, B (eds) (2014) *Contemporary Issues in the Early Years*. London: SAGE.

Rabinow, P (ed) (1984) *The Foucault Reader*. London: Penguin.

Rathus, S (2007) *Childhood: Voyages in Development*. London: Wadsworth.

Ridley, M (2003) *Nature via Nurture: Genes, Experience and What Makes Us Human*. London: Harper.

Wall, K (2006) *Special Needs and Early Years*. London: Paul Chapman Publishing.

5 The parented child

Learning outcomes:

- to examine the changing nature of parenting;

- to explore the importance of parenting and the pressures that parents face;

- to ask ourselves what a parent 'has' to do;

- to consider the role of government;

- to introduce the idea of partnership working with parents.

Critical questions

» *What is good parenting?*

» *Can practitioners teach good parenting?*

Introduction

Previously I have touched upon nature via nurture, arguing that while all children are conceived with a certain genetic makeup this is then influenced by how the child is looked after in the womb, and after birth as it grows up. I gave the examples of Yon (Chapter 3), a Romanian orphan, and Terry (Chapter 3), the child with psychosocial dwarfism, to demonstrate the impact that poor parenting can have upon the physical and psychological development of a child and the potential consequences. In both cases there was a happy ending demonstrating that good parenting does not only bring good outcomes but can also reverse poor developmental trends. Yet I also introduced the reader to Melanie, the young mother of Charlotte (Chapter 2). Melanie was a single mother with no immediate family for support and failed to feed Charlotte properly, I would argue through no fault of her own, but rather because of the bullying of professionals who supposedly knew best. Melanie's position reflects the growing involvement in childhood and childcare of practitioner views. On the one hand we have state intervention that quite rightly wants to protect children, but on the other hand a state that seems to think it knows best and should be telling parents what to do.

But what is a parent? Let us go back 30, maybe 40 years and ask ourselves this question. Surly then the answer was obvious. A parent was one half of a shared cultural and racial inheritance, a heterosexual married couple. If it was the man then the expectation was that he would go out to work and earn money to provide the family with shelter, clothes, food and a few luxuries. If it was the woman then she would stay at home, look after the home and nurture the children. There was an inevitability about the process by which you got to this arrangement, what would happen within it and how it would progress. Come forward to the beginning of the twenty-first century and how things have changed! Marriage is an institution in decline (interestingly, second marriages are on the increase) and we no longer talk about parenting as simply being undertaken by a couple as being a single parent after divorce or by choice is widespread. And what about the idea of being from a shared background, be it in terms of class or race? Yes, the majority of people still form relationships with people from their own background, but the barriers are breaking down as they are with sex and gender. The idea of gay couples, single parents, surrogacy, mixed-race couples and so forth would have been anathema to previous generations.

But what is 'good' parenting? When writing this chapter I asked myself: *Have I been a good parent?* My two children, both boys, now in their mid-twenties, are healthy, independent young men in work and as far as I can tell they are enjoying life. My assessment is that the outcome of my parenting is good and therefore I must have been a reasonably good parent. Correction, we (my wife and I) must have been good parents.

Critical reflection

» *Compare your parents with your own marital or otherwise situation. How have things changed?*

Parents and carers

It is the parents I feel sorry for. You are always a parent and I have been one for twenty-eight years. I sometimes breathe a sigh of relief that I have sons when I am at work or in the pub and I hear the angst of fathers with daughters. But perhaps I am being falsely smug, that my boys somehow have easier and safer lives than girls. I have already touched upon sex, body image, addiction, technology and education as pressures and conflicts and surely these impact upon both boys and girls.

Parents today are dealing with rebellious 'beasts' as never before, having lost the certainties of previous generations. Until the late 1950s and early 60s the norms of parenting and being a child had remained relatively stable since the turn of the century. For adults there was considerable uniformity in terms of when people married, the work they did, when they had children and how they raised them. Social and economic boundaries were in place and in general adhered to. For the child there were many markers and rites of passage that defined the journey from birth to infancy, to adolescence and into adulthood. These stages would be similar to the ones their parents had gone through: baptism, school, military service/college, stable employment and leaving home. Adults and children alike understood where they stood and where they were going. Also, the power within the parent–child relationship had not really changed for centuries, when children had no rights and families were in general left to get on with life.

Things have changed in just a few short decades. Childhood is now the site of conflicting pressures and much uncertainty. In education, for example, there is a stronger rhetoric of child-centeredness, but also a stronger role for early years schooling in producing human capital for an expanding economy. Increased calls for children to live their childhood fully are met by the public, if unreal, view that there are now few spaces where they can safely go alone. While children are perhaps over-protected from imagined risks they are exposed to others such as obesity. While these tensions are about children, they reside in adults; not the least significant aspect of our debates about childhood, indeed, is the way in which they re-focus and put in question our conceptions of adulthood itself.

Our children need to be cared for physically, intellectually and emotionally, but still need guiding without smothering the creative energy of youth. How can parents achieve that balance between care and control? Are we dealing with a creature that needs taming, or one that has been corrupted by society, or something in between? As we reached the end of the nineteenth century *Psychology... firmly colonized childhood in a pact with medicine, education and government agencies* (James et al, 1998, p 17), and began to offer some of what it thought were the answers through schooling and therapy, but are these fundamentally controlling rather than affirming? It is my contention that the tension between care and control in relation to children remains the ever-present and most important dynamic that individuals and society struggle to resolve, and this has not been helped by the emergence of risk and fear for our children's safety.

It is a paradox that at a time when British society has become prosperous with expanding choice and growing freedom there is an increased sense of risk. Could it be that we have more to lose? As Postman puts it, *Children are the living messages we send to a time we will not see* (Postman, 1994, p 23). He warns of a blurring between children's and adult concerns; Postman observes that mass media expose children to phenomena that they are not old enough to understand, such as violence, sex and death. Postman writes, *If all the secrets of adulthood are opened to children, cynicism, apathy or ignorance replace curiosity for them* (Postman, 1994, p 23). Yet we have advanced so fast we have gone beyond this and with the rapid growth of the global society not only has childhood changed irreversibly, but so has parenting and for many the child has become the must-have accessory. Certainly we have a society in which the child is seen to be vulnerable to a variety of threats, real and imagined, from which they need to be protected. This despite the fact that threats are comparatively rare: *people's personal experience is often at odds with this pessimistic picture and the anxieties about being at risk seem to be out of all proportion'* (Thompson, 2009, p 88). Of these risks, one appears to touch social consciousness above and beyond the others, the fear that our children will fall victim to a violent criminal act such as child abuse, rape, abduction and murder. In the next chapter on child abuse and significant harm I will discuss what happened at Little Ted's nursery in Plymouth and how tragedies such as this can influence public opinion and how the government have felt forced to get involved in feeding a child protection industry that continues to grow.

Alongside this we have heard more and more about the rights of the child, the child's voice, child-centredness and social competence and there is much cultural and legal advance in the direction of children's emancipation. The debate around physical chastisement has brought many of the issues to the fore: why shouldn't a parent have the right to smack their child?

The desired child

> We must be frank, we can't afford to look after the thousands of babies that are being orphaned every day,' says Miriam Nyirongo, a retired nurse who runs an orphanage in the northern city of Mzuzu. 'If rich people like Madonna take just one child, it will be a major boost for Malawi. People like Baby David, when they come to know their roots, might wish to do the same to others.
>
> (BBC News, 16 October 2006)

The decision by the pop singer Madonna to adopt an African child divided Malawi and worldwide opinion: *Maxwell Matewere, Executive Director of child rights group Eye of the Child, said his organisation is appealing to the government to reconsider the adoption. 'Madonna might have good intentions but we must follow the law to the letter to avoid a situation where criminals with money might take advantage to abuse our children,' he said* (BBC News, 16 October 2006).

Not so long ago having a child was regarded as a blessing, something God had given, over which we as humans had no control. If a couple could not have a child then they either accepted this or divorced. Sometimes children were stolen, traded, bought or informerly adopted. While in Britain there was no adoption legislation until the 1920s, adoption law has modernised with changing social attitudes and a greater focus on the rights of the child and continuing contact with the birth family. Social attitudes to childhood and child rearing have changed greatly during the last 50 years. Mothers no longer stay at home, fathers often take an active part in child rearing and the construction of the family has departed from the traditional design with single parents, single-sex parents and so forth.

What does a parent 'have' to do?

Opinions of what children need vary even between parents. Finding a general definition of children's needs and wants because of the social and cultural differences in the world may seem impossible. However, an internationally agreed document does exist, in which these wants and needs are set out. The Convention on the Rights of the Child is a set of standards

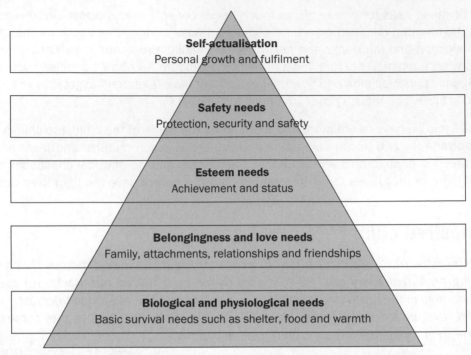

Figure 5.1 *Maslow's hierarchy of needs. Adapted from Mukherji, P and Dryden, L (2014).*

and obligations for the treatment of children that grew from the recognition that children have universal needs and that these can be defined. The Convention came into force in 1990 and has since been ratified by nearly all members of the United Nations.

One of the guiding principles of the Convention is the *best interests of the child*. In England and Wales we talk about the child being paramount (1989 Children Act). Building on current childcare knowledge it outlines a culturally independent picture of what children need to thrive. It presents the vision of a child as a human individual, and an intrinsic member of a family and community, who has specific needs if he or she is to become a happy and successful adult. The theoretical basis of this view is provided by Maslow in his hierarchy of needs, as displayed in Figure 5.1, and reflects the fundamental elements of what every child needs. In the early years these elements are most importantly provided by the parent.

As the chapters of this book highlight, we can distinguish between physical, mental, spiritual, moral and social needs. On a purely physical level children need an adequate standard of living and protection from physical danger in order that they may enjoy basic health and welfare. Psychological needs are defined as the need for education, leisure and recreational activities. Specifically mentioned is the need for schooling and literacy and access to information through books and a variety of media platforms.

Alongside the meeting of a child's basic needs, the child needs to be integrated into a stable community and family environment. He or she needs continuity of upbringing in a settled cultural background and with love – because this gives them the security they need for their development and develops their attachment. In this we recognise that psychological needs are as fundamental as physical needs if the child is to follow a positive developmental path to adulthood. In this respect Maslow's hierarchy of needs, which assumes that psychosocial needs such as safety, love and recognition need be addressed only after physiological needs have been met, is misleading. As we can see in respect to brain development and the consequences of this, mental, spiritual, moral and social needs of children are equally as important as their physical needs.

Critical question

»   *Take Erikson and Maslow together. Can we develop an integrated typology?*

While it is important for parents to keep children safe they also need to know when to let them be independent and even take risks. Children are driven to want to do things for themselves and where appropriate should be allowed to do so. This want can be fulfilled as soon as a child has attained a degree of personal independence. Parents teach their children to feed and dress themselves, which are early expressions of responsibility. Much of this learning is motivated by imitation and the example given by parents, siblings and practitioners. Parents also provide the first experiences of possessing and caring for their own objects. Responsibility is embedded in the framework and the limits that parents set for their children's experiences. Limits are necessary for practical reasons such as the physical safety of the child, but they are also essential to the learning of social skills such as controlling anger and the moral values of respect towards other beings and objects.

The framework and limits that parents impart on their children are the preconditions for living as a social and moral person. So the ultimate aim of parenting should be to help a child to grow up to be a productive, happy adult. We can identify four styles of parenting as follows:

* authorities parenting;

* authoritarian parenting;

* indulgent parenting;

* neglectful parenting.

One might argue that many parents can be each of these at different times and under different circumstances, but an authorities or neglectful parent is probably the one you do not want.

Parents in crisis

Drug and alcohol addiction, mental health difficulties, domestic violence, divorce and poverty are all issues that lead to parental crises, times when parents struggle to focus on the needs of the child. These issues can lead to neglect and abuse, but equally as practitioners we must make sure we do not jump to conclusions about the parenting ability of parents with these difficulties. The assessment should not focus on the parental difficulty, but rather on the parenting ability of the adults involved and how the difficulty may impact upon that ability. Problems can come from many different directions and circumstances.

Separation, divorce and the blended family

Forty per cent of all children experience parental separation and a third of families now include step-children. While society has become more tolerant and accepting of different forms of families, children are often casualties of parental break-up even if the adults involved are reasonably amicable. Babies and young children are complex and observe far more of what is going on within the family than might at first appear likely.

CASE STUDY

Melanie and David decided to live together. They both had children. Two weeks later they all moved in together. *We didn't sleep for the first 48 hours – and the first year could have been easier*, Melanie said. Bethan, David's daughter, settled down reasonably well. Elliot, Melanie's son and the youngest at two years of age, pushed David away at first. It took seven months before he would *let me hold him properly, but he still needed his dummy, so it was easy to baby him*. Peter, aged five and Melanie's other son, had lost trust in adults because his birth father did not want to see him. Melanie and David admitted later that they should have planned things better and discussed it with the children first. They realised that they should have built relationships between the five of them before rushing in together. It was what the adults wanted and they ignored the needs of the children.

Critical questions

»   *As practitioners we will often be working with blended families. How can we gain knowledge and understanding of the dynamics of such situations?*

»   *How do you feel about dummies?*

Older children are inevitably physically and psychologically caught up in the dynamics of family break-up. They develop views and opinions about who is and is not right and their wishes can be listened to, while younger children may not appear to be so involved. But they are.

Babies and young children sense change and while they may not understand it they are aware it is happening. Attachments are disrupted, routines are altered and physical and emotional strands in the child's life are generally disrupted. It is often the case that settings such as the nursery or reception class are the only things that provide continuity.

When it comes to the new, blended family the impact on children can be significant and damaging. If the adults, often caught up in their own complex emotions, fail to recognise this practitioners need to be on alert. Losing a birth parent, gaining a step-parent along with step-brothers and sisters can be disruptive, threatening and damaging. While the new adult couple may be happy the dynamics between the newly formed child grouping can be far from happy. Children in the early years may appear to be less aware, but they are aware. Practitioners need to be able to work with this either individually with the child or in a particular setting. The practitioner may also become involved in contact arrangement, with one parent delivering the child to the setting and another collecting them. The practitioner may be called as a witness in family proceedings as they are in regular contact with the child, see the family and are expected to have expert knowledge and understanding. This is another occasion when the importance of the practitioner's understanding of the link between theory and practice comes to the fore. The court will expect the practitioner to make these links.

The Children and Families Act 2014 requires parents in dispute to consider mediation as a means of settling that dispute rather than litigation by making attendance at a mediation information and assessment meeting a statutory prerequisite to starting court proceedings. This may enable couples to manage a break-up of their relationship in a child-focused way.

Adoption

Adoption in Britain can be a controversial subject. How do we make certain children are going to the 'right' parents, but at the same time make the process efficient for those involved? The Children and Families Act 2014 is an attempt to respond to these challenges and improve things for both children and adoptive parents. The Act proposes major changes to adoption procedures, in particular preventing local authorities delaying an adoption to find the perfect match if there are other suitable adopters available. The ethnicity of a child and prospective adopters will come second, in most cases, to the speed of placing a child with good parents in a permanent home. The proposals were originally set out in the Adoption Action Plan published in March 2012 – part of wider reforms to speed up and overhaul the system for prospective adoptive parents and children.

There are also changes proposed for family law such as creating a time limit of six months, by which time care cases must be completed, and making it explicit that case-management decisions should be made only after impacts on the child, their needs and timetable have been considered. These include getting rid of unnecessary processes in family proceedings by removing the requirement for interim care and supervision orders to be renewed every month by the judge, and instead allowing the judge to set the length and renewal requirements of interim orders for a period which he or she considers appropriate.

Once the child is adopted practitioners should be aware of the issues that might impact upon the child and should focus on the 'belongingness' definition of a family, rather than on the circumstances surrounding a particular child's birth and parenting. In the case of adoption in Britain, all adoptive children are given a photographic record of their life so far with pictures of parents and so forth. Photographs might be used in the early years setting or the classroom as an introduction to a general discussion on the nature and form of families. Such related activities, however, can stimulate thought about who we are and where we come from, bring our feelings about our families to the surface, help us to look at our families from a different perspective and make our families more visible to others. In the case of children who have been adopted, this reflection may result in confusion, raise questions that cannot be answered, and underline differences between these children and their peers. Practitioners need to be balanced in these matters and this approach is true when it comes to any difference or diversity. Also, it is worth being aware that the worker himself may be carrying issues from childhood that need to be reflected upon before exposure to the setting.

CASE STUDY

Aaron

Three months after being approved by the adoption panel, the couple still had not heard anything so they subscribed to 'Be My Parent', which shows the children available nationally, not just in the immediate local authority. In there they saw a picture of Aaron and immediately decided that was the child for them.

Aaron was nearly six and came from a traumatising and abusive family background. Things moved very quickly. The day after his sixth birthday, in 2012, Aaron became their son. A year later the adoption was finalised. The whole thing took two-and-a-half years. But if they had wanted a 'different kind' of child it would have taken a lot longer. Newborn babies are rarely put up for adoption and there are few infants. The majority are older and from troubled backgrounds or disabled.

Aaron came from an extreme background of neglect and violent physical abuse. He'd had to move foster placements because of his behaviour, and had a statement of special educational needs, so the couple knew he was not going to be the easiest child to bring up. The social worker warned the couple but they thought, *He just needs a stable home and he'll be fine*.

Aaron at times can be a difficult little boy to live with. The couple feels strongly that social services need to be more open about the children who are available to be adopted, but the social worker would say that the couple were not open to listening as they were so desperate for a child.

Social services provided therapeutic input and Aaron made an attachment with the couple, but still finds it very hard to relate to anybody and is very fearful; an angry shout and he still freezes with fear.

Critical reflection

Our society is becoming steadily more diverse, not only with a growing mix of cultures, but also with the changing shape of families. It is important that practitioners are willing and able to help young children develop an awareness of and appreciation for the many kinds of family structures in today's society. Early years practitioners can strive to provide play and teaching materials and experiences that celebrate diversity and the interrelatedness of cultures by including images of families whose members do not necessarily share the same features.

» *Does the setting you work in, or the ones you visit, follow this type of approach?*

The military, bereavement and critical illness

Over the last 15 years Britain has been involved in a number of conflicts, in particular Iraq I, Iraq II and Afghanistan. Many hundreds of young men and women have been killed in these conflicts, several thousands have been seriously injured and unknown numbers have returned physically unharmed but suffering from Post-Traumatic Stress Disorder (PTSD). This condition, through no fault of their own, can have the same impact on a family as any of the conditions or situations mentioned above. PTSD can display itself in many ways, numbing emotions, stimulating outbursts of temper and creating false reality. The impact on a family can be serious.

CASE STUDY

Sophie

Sophie was the four-year-old daughter of Captain Louise and Duncan Hammon. The nursery had noticed Sophie was unusually quiet on Monday morning and recorded this in her notes. On Wednesday a member of staff saw a hand-shaped bruise on her thigh. Sophie's key worker thought it looked like a hand mark. The worker knew Sophie well and asked the child how she had got the bruise. Sophie looked down and in a very quiet voice said, *I made Mummy very angry*. The worker told the nursery manager who rang social services.

Sophie's mother Louise was a captain in the Royal Engineers and had been based at Camp Bastion in Afghanistan for six months. She had recently returned from there. A social worker and plain-clothed female police officer visited the school and talked with Sophie. The social worker telephoned Duncan Hammon for him to come into school while the police officer contacted the interview suite to arrange for them to take Sophie there. In the meantime another police officer was on her way to visit Louise Hammon at the army camp.

Critical reflection

The Hammons are a family that are clearly in crisis. However we feel about what Louise may or may not have done, or what may have made her act in the way she did, we need to look at the whole family. All families go through periods of crisis, some minor and some major, and practitioners and services need to be flexible and understanding enough to work with this. This does not mean that we should excuse abusive behaviour, but be prepared to work with it, as we will consider in the next chapter where we will also hear more about Sophie and her family.

» *Can you understand why people under stress abuse?*

Military families, especially at a time of war, are always aware that a loved one may be killed or seriously injured. This can happen to anyone, not only to people in the military, and the consequences for all involved can be traumatic. The sudden death of a parent is traumatic for the family and the children, and practitioners need to be able to respond. As practitioners we need to recognise that serious illness is as much of a loss as a death.

CASE STUDY

Mark is 37 and has cancer. He is married to Jenny and they have two children, a son aged ten and a daughter Tabitha aged four. Tabitha is aware that her father is ill, but has no idea how seriously ill he is. She does know that Daddy is no longer the father she used to know. He no longer plays with her and does not laugh anymore. She knows Mummy cries a lot and that her brother keeps shouting and running off. She knows that her key worker at the nursery is always smiley and happy, plays with her and is always there. Tabitha wants to go and live with her key worker.

Critical reflection

» *How do you feel about death?*

» *How would you explain death and serious illness to children in the early years?*

Parenting and state intervention

In the case of Sophie Hammon we can understand why the authorities became involved, to protect Sophie, but the government has increasingly become involved in the day-to-day lives of children and parenting. We have previously discussed medical issues and the role of education. Childhood and parenting was never a political issue and vote-winning platform before the 'discovery' of child abuse in the sixties and seventies. Even then child abuse was very much seen as something those in poverty or with mental health or psychopathic tendencies carried out. During the course of the book so far I have raised the issue of parental choice and how the government, media and professionals attempt to influence our parenting. There is no doubt that the state has increasingly become involved in directing how children should or should not be reared. In Britain between 2003 and 2010 the government introduced substantial policies and procedures under the Every Child Matters agenda. The Labour government of the time perceived the need to activate an agenda to improve things for children, partly because of the tragic death of seven-year-old Victoria Climbié in 2000. The Every Child Matters agenda highlighted five outcomes for children, as follows:

- children should be healthy;
- children should stay safe;
- children should enjoy life and achieve;
- children should make a positive contribution to society;
- children should have economic well-being.

One cannot argue with these basic expectations for children and they fit with the Convention. It serves the purpose of the government to protect children not only for ethical and humanitarian reasons, but also for providing a healthy workforce for the future. Government intervention is fundamentally discriminatory in that it can assume that parents living in poverty, single parents and parents with limited learning are not going to be good parents. This feeds into the populist discriminatory rhetoric that we have observed during recent years, cantering on the perverse scroungers v workers debate.

Current coalition government thinking appears to want to support the 'traditional' family while not discriminating against single parents, gay and lesbian couples and so forth. While the number of nuclear families containing married parents is declining, the government has persisted with the notion that this is still best for children and social stability in general, for instance by awarding tax breaks to those that are married.

CASE STUDY

Patrick and Susan

Patrick is a single parent working as a shop assistant on the minimum wage. He leaves his daughter Susan, aged five, at the breakfast club before going to work and picks her up after school. He does receive benefits and Susan gets free school meals. Despite his best efforts he and Susan are isolated with few social contacts beyond work and school and no free money to spend on treats. The head teacher has referred Susan as *a child in need* to social services, but Patrick refuses any help.

Critical reflection

Patrick is not doing anything 'wrong', but is struggling to give Susan the quality of life he would like. He is proud and believes that human rights give him the right to refuse help, however well meant. Human rights can, of course, be argued both ways – rights in terms of freedom from state intervention, but also rights as entitlement to state intervention and support if needed. In Patrick's case one can argue that Susan's rights as a child outweigh her father's right to reject the help on offer, that the needs of the child are paramount. A problem for Patrick might be that he feels patronised, even ashamed of not being able to provide for his daughter.

» *How do we work with Patrick?*

Government policy is at risk of punishing parents that want to do the best they can. Humanistic sources would argue that we need to see the people first before the money. This would mean a more radical edge to supporting families rather than the populist attitude towards welfarism that we currently have.

Critical reflection

Striking a balance between government intervention and civil liberties is often very difficult.

» *To what extent should central government or local authorities intervene in people's private life? To protect a child of course, but to tell a parent how to parent?*

» *How does government intervention impact upon your life?*

Parental partnerships

The idea of involving parents in decision making about medicine, education and social care is comparatively new. Not so long ago we saw the doctor, teacher or social worker as the expert, but times have changed and we have become more cynical about such people. There is now rightly an expectation that parents and children should be involved in making decisions about them as individuals, but also about the organisations and settings to which they go.

Researchers, practitioners and policymakers recognise the importance of parental involvement. They recognise that when parents participate in their children's care and education, the result is an improvement in the way children settle into the setting, play with other children and increase their learning. Increased attendance, fewer disciplinary problems and higher aspirations have also been correlated with an increase in parental involvement, even after socio-economic status and student ability have been taken into account. Furthermore, increased parental involvement creates the perception that the school is more effective and successful.

More recent understandings of the ways in which young children learn recognise the child as an 'active learner', relying on and learning from a wide range of experiences beyond the school boundary. Viewing children as active learners highlights that not all learning takes place in school and we have already talked about the vital role parents play in developing the growing child. There is a consensus of opinion that much of children's early literacy and numeracy development happens outside formal learning and occurs within the social context of the home, family and community. If the early years setting can establish positive partnerships with parents it can help all children, but in particular those that might be struggling socially and/or educationally. In this way, parents benefit as well as their children if they are seen as having a role in their children's education. They develop a greater appreciation of their role, an improved sense of self-worth, stronger social networks, and even the desire to continue their own education.

Whilst the literature provides evidence for the benefits of involving parents in their children's education, it also demonstrates the problems that practitioners have in working with parents as partners, especially those whom they see as different, including those from minority ethnic groups and those in poverty. These hard-to-reach parents may themselves have struggled at school and be tentative in their interactions with teachers, and this may leave parents with the feeling that teachers do not seem to understand what they were saying. Practitioners need to make the extra effort to reach out to these parents, for instance through home visits, the use of interpreters and an understanding of the parents' lifestyle and culture. The most important thing is to be able to make time to build relationships and trust. This is obviously easier said than done when practitioners are so busy with the day-to-day tasks of running and working within their setting. It is made more difficult if the parent or parents are seen to be 'difficult' and/or are unreliable.

CASE STUDY

Rosie

Rosie is the two-year-old daughter of travellers Dora and Sean O'Brien. Neither Dora nor Sean had much formal education and neither can read. Both, however, want more for Rosie. They live in a caravan and move every few months in search of work for Sean so it is not possible for Rosie to remain in any one nursery for long.

Critical reflection

» *As an early years practitioner how would you manage the above?*

Conclusion

To become a parent is perhaps one of, if not the most challenging thing any of us will have to do. It affects everything we do and hope to do. To many it is the most incredible thing we ever do while to others it can become loathsome.

The essential role of parents in fulfilling children's needs stems from the decisive influence of the first years of life for a child's intellectual, emotional and moral development. Love is probably the most elementary and important need. However, it eludes scientific definition and is hardly measurable objectively. Security in the non-material sense is also difficult to describe, but as practitioners we have to assess these things if we are to work effectively with families and sometimes protect children.

Summary

In this chapter I have sought to place parenting in its modern context, discuss the challenges faced by parents and explore the importance of parenting and the pressures that they face. We have considered what parents 'have' to do and then considered the concept of partnership between practitioners and parents and how important this is in working with all families, but in particular those that are hard to reach. As we have done on a number of occasions during the book we have looked at the role of government.

Critical reflection

» *Consider why people decide to become parents or not. Think about the pressures that are placed on people to have children and how we as a society still view childless people with suspicion, or even pity.*

» *Reflect on your own attitudes to different family structures.*

Critical reflection

The Children and Families Act 2014 is an important piece of legislation that should change the way in which families interact with services and the courts. I will briefly discuss this in the conclusion, but do your own research. How important do you think it will be?

Taking it further

Horwath, J (2010) *The Child's World*. London: Jessica Kingsley.

Kübler-Ross, E and Kessler, D (2005) *On Grief and Grieving: Finding the Meaning of Grief through the Five Stages of Loss.* London: Simon & Schuster.

Lindon, J (2012) *Understanding Child Development 0–8 Years*. London: Hodder Education.

Page, J, Clare, A and Nutbrown, C (2013) *Working with Babies and Children*. London: SAGE.

Ward, U (2013) *Working with Parents*. London: SAGE.

References

James, A, Jenks, C and Prout, A (1998) *Theorizing Childhood*. Cambridge: Polity.

Mukherji, P and Dryden, L (eds) (2014) *Foundations of Early Childhood*. London: SAGE.

Postman, N (1994) *The Disappearance of Childhood*. London: Penguin.

Thompson, N (2009) *People Skills*. London: Palgrave Macmillan.

6   Children with special educational needs and disability

Learning outcomes:

*   to examine what SEN and disability are;

*   to consider discrimination and inclusion;

*   to consider the health and well-being of the disabled child and how we can support children to achieve good outcomes;

*   to consider the role of the early years practitioner and services in working with children and parents.

Critical question

»   *At a time when resources are scarce agencies have to make difficult decisions about allocating resources. So what is disability?*

Introduction

There is a danger in deciding to have a separate chapter on children with disabilities. It could be seen as discriminatory, separating a child with a disability from other children, adding a label that can be damaging and regressive. This said, there is no doubt that a child with a disability or with special educational needs does have extra and/or different needs. Disability in the early years of a child's life presents its own complex and particularly challenging issues for the child, parents, siblings and practitioners. This chapter will not attempt to cover all the relevant areas or provide a comprehensive guide for working with children with special educational needs and disability. There are many good texts in circulation that achieve this. In this chapter I will consider a limited number of issues that fit with the general themes in this book.

The birth of a disabled child can be shattering for parents. We all expect to have perfectly healthy children and to be told there might be or is something wrong comes as a shock. Not only does it change our expectations of the child, but it also dramatically changes the future we imagined we might have as a family. Having a disabled child changes lives and the impact cannot be underestimated, creating stress and disharmony in family relationships, but it also has financial and lifestyle implications. Siblings, for instance, are often 'forgotten' as all the attention is focused on the child with the disability and it is vitally important that parents and practitioners remember all the children in the family.

CASE STUDY

Amanda, Part 3

In Chapters 1 and 2 we met Amanda and her parents Jenny and Simon. Amanda had cystic fibrosis. A nursery place had been found for Amanda and this gave Jenny and Simon some respite, but they were struggling as a couple. Jenny did not want sex and financially things were becoming difficult. Jenny continued to blame herself for Amanda's condition and then one day Simon told her he was leaving.

Critical reflection

Think about the challenges any single parent may struggle with, but for Jenny things may be even more difficult.

» *What are the risk factors here?*

Poverty remains a serious problem within society. There are no easy solutions to this and a succession of governments has struggled to resolve the problem of children living in poverty. A disabled child living in poverty presents significant problems for all those involved. Practitioners have a responsibility, as part of a commitment to children's well-being, to ensure that families are aware of their eligibility for services and benefits. Families with children with disabilities often live more impoverished lives and are often significantly more indebted than the rest of the population. They are less likely to own their own home, and thus hold no capital with which to decrease the cost of borrowing. Given the long-established link between low socio-economic status and poor health outcomes, it is easy to see how families become trapped by disability into a cycle of poverty and worsening health. At this extremity, poverty is unarguably a menace to health, and therefore a concern for the health sector. Children within these family units are often vulnerable to neglect and abuse.

CASE STUDY

Chelsea and Lorraine

Lorraine is a 22-year-old single mother. She has a four-year-old daughter called Chelsea who has learning difficulties. Lorraine and Chelsea live in a local authority flat in a high-rise block. Chelsea is subject to a statement of special educational needs and Lorraine receives benefits for this. Chelsea attends the local nursery five weekday mornings. The nursery has been very welcoming and supportive of both Chelsea and her mother. Chelsea has a social worker who visits once a month.

Lorraine has no family living close by and few local friends. Apart from when Chelsea is at the nursery she is never out on her own. She has not been clubbing or on a date since Chelsea was born. There is no local respite care available. All she can see is the rest of her life stretching monotonously ahead of her. She feels isolated and is possibly depressed. Lorraine loves Chelsea, but is thinking of asking social services to take her into care *to give me my life back*.

Critical reflection

» *As a practitioner how would you engage with Chelsea and Lorraine?*

Every parent, of course, has the right to protect and get the best for their children, but this may mean that another child is disenfranchised in some way. Does the need of one child trump the need of another? It should not, but it can. I referred in the critical question at the beginning of this chapter to scarce resources, so decisions have to be made by agencies, but decisions are made in society every day about who gets what and disability remains an obstruction. Disabled children and young people should enjoy the same rights and opportunities as other children, and should be fully included in every part of the community in which the family live. One of my students has undertaken research into play park access for disabled children in Chichester, Sussex. Carrie is an experienced respite carer for disabled children and has significant experience of taking disabled children to play parks and similar places where all children enjoy going. Her research demonstrates beyond challenge that none of the play parks surveyed were suitable for disabled children (Prior, 2014). This research is transferable to most boroughs in England and Wales and probably the rest of the UK. Providing children with disabilities with the best possible start in life is vitally important, but outcomes for children with disabilities remain poor.

Defining SEN and disability

What is normal? An important question when you hear it used so often in respect to the care and education of children. One obvious answer to the question is there is no such thing as normal and all children beyond the biological are different, individual and deserve to be treated as such. We have standard methods of assessment and measurement against which to measure a child's development during the early years:

- gross motor;

- fine motor;

- speech and language;

- personal/social.

These measures imply that there is a 'normal' against which we view children, for instance centile charts are regularly used by health visitors to assess a child's progress. The term 'special needs', like the word 'normal', is open to interpretation. All children have needs, physical and psychological, and these needs vary. We have to find ways and means to define what we actually mean.

The 1989 Children Act states that any child with a disability is a child in need, but does little to advance our definition or understanding any further. The Equality Act 2010 states that a disabled person is someone who has a *physical or mental impairment which has a substantial and long-term adverse effect on his or her ability to carry out normal day-to-day activitie*s. The important point about this definition is that it makes no reference to the origin of these difficulties, nor any attempt to exclude particular conditions. So children with dyslexia, anorexia nervosa, or cystic fibrosis are, therefore, all labelled as disabled (although may not see themselves as such), and have a right to protection under the Act. The definition makes the important point that disability is a broad category, not limited to what have traditionally been regarded as 'disabled children', i.e. those with physical and/or educational limitations. It also views 'day to day activities' as important, recognising that 'disabled' children want and should be able to do everything any other child can do, but also uses this controversial word 'normal' without defining what 'normal' is.

We also have to try to be clear about the differences and similarities between the terms special educational needs and disability. There are similarities, not least in the way society and the educational and care systems can label children with any condition that falls within these categories. In this chapter I will tend to use the word disabled or disability to cover all the children that fall within these categories. In doing so I appreciate that this in itself may be discriminatory and not allow for difference, but it is a pragmatic decision.

Models of disability

Traditionally the health model for disability has been the one that practitioners have taken as the measure against which we assess children. The model is limiting in that it concentrates on the diagnosable condition of the child and does not have universal acceptance, and nor should it because it is limited and limiting to the child, to the family and to the services available. The social model of disability regards disability as a social construct, existing only as a result of the broader society's failure to accommodate difference. This has generated much debate, but sheds little light on our need for a definition. But then do we need a definition, and if so why? Ideally every child in our society would get the things they need. Any vulnerable child would get the protection they need, but we do not live in an ideal world. Our purpose in defining disability is to allow us to identify children within the population of all children who are in need of additional assistance, in order to improve their quality of life and prospects. So is it really all about resources? We simply do not have the resources to provide all children with exactly what they need and we therefore have to make judgements. Does this child need assistance or not? In relation to services managers often have to make decisions between children. Most social services departments will have criteria against which they assess each case.

With severe and complex disabilities we often hear discussion about the quality of life. Quality of life at the serious end of disability can be an area of tension between parents, healthcare and the law. A number of cases have brought the issue to the public attention, such as the one in the case study below.

CASE STUDY

Charlotte

Charlotte Wyatt was born in October 2003 at St Mary's Hospital, Portsmouth, at only 26 weeks, weighing just 1lb. During the six months following her birth she stopped breathing three times and had severe disabilities – she was deaf and blind, had brain damage and had serious organ failure. The NHS took the decision that they did not want to resuscitate her if she stopped breathing again, as they believed she had no quality of life. However, Charlotte's parents, Debbie and Darren, did not agree with this decision. In most cases like this, parents and medical staff can come to an agreement over the best course of action for the child. However, no consensus could be reached here, and so the Wyatts went to the High Court to ask a judge to decide whether Charlotte had a legal right to be kept alive. The Judge said:

> In reaching my view, I have of course been informed by the medical evidence as to the prospects to her of aggressive treatment. I hope I have looked much wider than that and seen not just a physical being but the body, mind and spirit expressed in a human personality of unique worth who is profoundly precious to her parents. It is for that personality of unique worth that I have striven to discern her best interests. It is my one regret that my search has led to a different answer than that sought by these parents.

He went on to say that all the evidence showed that Charlotte would have a terrible quality of life: *I do not believe any further aggressive treatment, even if necessary to prolong life, is in her best interests. I know that may mean she may die earlier than otherwise she might have done but in my judgement the moment of her death will only be slightly advanced.*

The Wyatt family decided not to appeal the decision.

Arguably, any child with a disability will have their quality of life affected with ongoing medical care, practitioner intrusion, social limitations and discrimination.

Critical reflection

As science progresses and we keep more severely disabled children with complex needs alive, local authorities struggle to allocate resources to cases. One case can swallow many tens of thousands of pounds, money that might be spread amongst several cases.

» *How do we as a society make these decisions?*

Discrimination and inclusion

A debate that has been present within education and care for many years is what is best for the child with a disability, to segregate them in a 'special' school that has all the necessary resources in one place or integrate them into the mainstream system. I believe there are arguments for both courses of action. When it comes to severely disabled children, needing detailed care or resources, I believe the argument swings towards the specially equipped school, so it is at the middle and end of the disability spectrum where the decision is less clear-cut.

Placing children with similar disabilities in the one place can be labelling, isolates them from other children and inhibits their ability to become part of the social life of those other children. Yet placing a child even with a 'mild' disability in amongst so-called 'normal' children can lead to bullying and isolation. The idea behind inclusion is that a setting, for instance a care home or school, structures itself so that all children are embraced and are treated equally. The idea of inclusion is very much based around the social model of disability, in that it is society that segregates and not the condition itself and therefore society needs to change in order to make certain all children are treated equally, for instance by making certain that school corridors are wide enough for wheelchairs. Physical change is comparatively straightforward, but it is the psychological where the toughest barriers exist.

The disabled child in the early years faces a number of challenges not only from their own circumstances, but also from the environment and the other children and adults around them. Despite changes in the law and a growing awareness and understanding amongst the public, discrimination against those with a disability remains an issue.

CASE STUDY

Darius

Darius is three years of age and has mild learning difficulties. He attends the local nursery. The nursery and staff are well aware of Darius' needs and work in partnership with his parents to meet them. He has been attending for over a year with no significant problems emerging for him, the staff or the other children. Darius has a favourite toy bear who lives at the nursery and every day when he comes in, he fetches the bear and keeps it all morning until he goes home at lunchtime. He is happy to leave the bear because *bear lives at nursery*. Other children in the group have learned to respect Darius' relationship with the bear and one girl, Mary, even brings the bear to Darius when he arrives and the three of them will play together. Then Simon, also three, arrives at the nursery and seeing the bear takes it before either Mary or Darius can get it. Upset and frustrated, Darius hits Simon in the face and Mary pushes Simon over.

Simon has a small bruise on his cheek and when his mother arrives to collect him the nursery manager explains what has happened. Simon's mother is furious and demands that social services be contacted and that Darius be expelled or she will take Simon away from the nursery. Leaving the office, the manager hears her telling other mothers what has happened and what a dangerous child Darius is.

Critical reflection

» *If you were the manager/owner of the nursery how would you manage the above?*

Child disability services

The majority of children with a disability have what we might call a 'mild' disability, a condition that requires relatively few resources, with a much smaller group of children with profound disability. We have an overall picture of the pattern of need: a large number of children requiring ongoing help, guidance and support, and a smaller group requiring more intensive intervention such as with the provision of medical and mobility equipment and even full-time care such as in the case of Charlotte Wyatt. When we are dealing with this diversity of need it is vital that services are co-ordinated so they can offer the very best in support not only to the child but also to the parents and siblings. Here we need to remember that many children, even young children, play an active role in caring for siblings, not to mention those that care for one or both of their parents. For all groups, such help needs to be co-ordinated between the various welfare agencies, in particular social services, health and education.

The variation and overlap within and between diagnoses require assessment and intervention to be broad and personalised. All aspects of the child and their circumstances need to be assessed be they physical, psychological or behavioural. Such assessment complexity places an obvious burden on practitioners and services in general. This burden has increased since survival rates have risen and we have become better at keeping children alive, for instance in the case of very premature babies. Indeed, there is an increasingly large group with intensive medical needs, primarily as a result of improved survival rates. Scientific progress in this field has been significant, as has the training and practice of medical and nursing staff. At the same time, and possibly because of modern life, we find new conditions to label such as ADHD, for which resources have to be found. Given these factors, it is easy to see how the demands for child disability services have increased dramatically in the last decade and consequently so has the pressure on services to make difficult decisions.

CASE STUDY

Amanda, Part 4

With Simon gone Jenny has been left with the full-time care of Amanda. Simon continues to support Jenny and Amanda financially and takes Amanda for contact twice a week. The social worker is aware of the situation and refers Jenny to a local support group. Jenny, however, does not drive and the support group is 45 minutes away. The social worker's manager decides that while the authority will pay the weekly fee for Jenny and Amanda to attend the support group they will not pay for or provide transport.

During supervision the manager candidly tells the social worker that while one can argue it is about sharing responsibility with the parent, even empowering the parent to contribute and not become reliant on services, it is actually about the allocation of resources.

The social worker is left to explain the situation to Jenny.

Critical reflection

The practitioner may often find themselves caught between the hopes and expectations of the family and the policy and procedures of the agency.

» *How would you use supervision with a manager to engage with these issues?*

The role of voluntary groups and charities cannot be underestimated when it comes to caring for disabled children and supporting families. In general they do an exceptional job with limited resources. These groups are just as much a part of the welfare market place as the many private companies and local authority departments that provide care. One of the complaints many parents have is that the carer allocated to their child keeps changing and there is a lack of consistency. On the other side of the argument, carers will say how poorly paid they are and how they are allocated inadequate time per young person to properly build relationships and provide quality care. There is no doubt that these issues have come about as a result of limited resources and possibly because of the opening up of welfare to market forces.

All practitioners working with children should be willing and able to work with practitioners from other agencies and, as with safeguarding, it is essential when working with disability that there is inter-agency co-operation.

Within child disability services the practitioner is more often than not focusing on improving the child's functioning and quality of life rather than treating the disability directly. The problems encountered are very often common to all, such as behaviour, sleep and feeding problems for the child and, as already mentioned, financial problems for the family. Secondly, the care of disabled children and families is complex, requiring contributions from social care, health and education and it is vital that services are as streamlined as possible for families to access. The introduction of the Children and Families Act 2014 means that government is charged with delivering better support for families by improving how vulnerable children receive the provision and help they need. So for instance the Act is expected to introduce a single, simpler assessment process for children with special educational needs or disabilities, supported by new education, health and care plans.

Parental partnerships

In the previous chapter we talked at length about parents and parenting and that chapter is relevant to work with all parents, but parental partnerships with parents with a disabled child can be extremely complex, long term and involve significant amounts of financial support. As

Kate Wall (2006, pp 70–1) points out, while parents may be committed to the needs of their child, they may not be so keen to work with the agencies offering help. Indeed the agencies may be seen as a threat or as having failed the child in some way. Even if these barriers are overcome the social worker or care manager can find himself or herself in several roles as family support, financial gatekeeper and more, and sometimes the child can get 'forgotten'. The literature and research would support the view that disabled children are probably more likely to suffer abuse than other particular groups of children. They are vulnerable, may have communication difficulties and parents can become frustrated and stressed with providing demanding long-term care. The practitioner, therefore, needs to be willing to be able to play with a disabled child as much as any child.

As I have discussed above, there can be a number of services involved with the family and not only is it vitally important for these services to be co-ordinated from a management point of view, but also that the services communicate, that the nursery worker is as well informed about the child's needs and plans as the social worker or the paediatrician. Even if the diagnosis is the same, survival rates, complication rates, healthcare needs, family support and so forth are all different.

Communication of course must include the parent; indeed the parent and child should be at the centre of assessment and planning. Every disabled child is different and services are not always designed with children in mind, or with the involvement of children and families and therefore it is vital that children and parents have their say and that they are listened to. Sometimes parents have to be proactive and assertive to get their voices heard, something that some will struggle with while for others, those who are more confident, it will come naturally. Practitioners in one agency should be willing to help parents have their say, even if it is uncomfortable for another agency to hear. It is often the case that practitioners in, for example, a nursery do not 'sit at the top table' when it comes to decision making and planning, but they can be a force when it comes to working in partnership with parents to bring about change and get things done. After all, it is the nursery workers, the carer, the teacher and so forth that have the regular day-to-day contact with parents and children.

Conclusion

It is important to remember that all children with disabilities are children first and that the disability is something to be managed in order to allow that child to have as full and fulfilling a life as possible. We have not attempted to define or discuss quality of life issues here, partly because they are fraught with ethical and moral dilemmas on which we will all have an opinion, but at the severe end of the disability spectrum it is a factor for all practitioners to be aware of. Scientific advances and improvements in healthcare have meant that more children than ever before are surviving serious disability and living for longer. There is an increase in the number of technology-dependent children in our society. This positive development, however, places pressure on families to continue caring for children with complex needs and on the authorities to find the resources to support and care for them.

All practitioners need to do their utmost to make certain that the families they work with understand what services are available, and feel empowered to make their voices heard. Early years practitioners are in an ideal position to support families in their relationships with medical, educational and social services, to make certain they receive the services and benefits they are entitled to. This does not mean that early years practitioners have to be experts, but rather that they recognise the issues and know where to signpost parents. Both parents and practitioners should also seek opportunities to build the partnership.

Summary

In this chapter we have examined the basics of special educational need and disability and the pressures that impose themselves on children and families, the role of services and the importance that the voice of the child and parent are heard and listened to. We have briefly considered the legislation and highlighted the promise of the 2013 Child and Families Act.

Critical reflection

» *Setting aside the formal definitions, what do you think disability is?*

» *How do you feel about ADHD? Does it exist, or is it simply a label for children with a variety of behavioural difficulties?*

» *Reflect on your own attitudes to difference and disability. Would you say you are always objective?*

Taking it further

I would enthusiastically recommend the books of Kate Wall. Written by a practitioner and academic, the writing places the child at the centre and recognises the challenges faced by both parents and practitioners. See also:

Ajay, S and Cockerel, H (2014) *Mary Sheridon's Birth to Five Years: Children's Developmental Progress*. London: Routledge.

Frederickson, N and Cline, T (2009) *Special Educational Needs, Inclusion and Diversity*. Maidenhead: Open University Press.

Pugh, G and Duffy, B (eds) (2014) *Contemporary Issues in the Early Years*. London: SAGE.

Wall, K (2009) *Autism and Early Years Practice*. London: SAGE.

References

Prior, C (2014) *Barriers Children and their Families Encounter when Accessing Play Provision in Chichester*. Chichester University Library.

Wall, K (2006) *Special Needs and Early Years: A Practitioner's Guide*. London: SAGE.

7 Abuse and significant harm

Learning outcomes:

*   to explore the background to current thinking on child abuse and child protection;
*   to consider the signs and symptoms of abuse;
*   to consider inter-agency working and the role of key agencies;
*   to introduce the importance of early intervention;
*   to examine the challenges of working with a family in which there has been abuse.

Critical question

» *Consider where the line is between the rights of parents to parent their children as they wish and the societal view of what is abuse. Abuse can be obvious with clear injuries or signs of neglect, but much of what is called abuse is less clear and open to interpretation.*

Introduction

One might have called this chapter 'the systemised child' because society has given itself to developing structures and systems in response to discovering child abuse in the 60s and 70s and a series of child deaths that have occurred on a regular basis since. The link between poverty, neglect and cruelty was made during the nineteenth century and for much of the twentieth century this fundamentally class-driven dynamic remained the main issue for concern. Society, through government, had reacted to protect children with legislation since 1889, when the first act of parliament for the prevention of cruelty to children was passed. The Children Act 1908 followed – establishing juvenile courts – and then in 1909 the Punishment of Incest Act made sexual abuse within families a matter for state jurisdiction rather than intervention by the clergy. It was through physiology, however, during the 60s, that child abuse as we know it was 'discovered'. With the improvement in X-ray medical practitioners began to see unusual or unexplained fractures. At first some attempted to explain these by hypothesising new bone diseases before Silverman (Humphries and Gully, 1999) demonstrated that they were in fact the result of unrecognised skeletal trauma. These initial observations culminated with the first description of the Battered-Child Syndrome in 1962 (Kempe, Silverman et al, 1962).

Once the issue had been exposed there followed a rapid growth in society's awareness of the scope of the problem of abuse. Since these revelations Anglo-Saxon society has pursued the archaeology of child abuse and the construction of a child protection machine. As society began to recognise these issues so it began to categorise, label, diagnose and register the children and their parents. The Children Act 1989 gave every child the right to protection from abuse and exploitation and the right to have inquiries made to safeguard their welfare. Its central tenet was that children are usually best looked after within their family.

Sadly it was often the tragedies and extremes that challenged thinking and encouraged people to examine that which seemed so normal as to be almost invisible. In Britain in 1974 it was the inquiry into the death of Maria Colwell at the hands of her step-father that highlighted a serious lack of co-ordination within child protection services and led to further changes in the system and a widening in the scope of identification and intervention. Nowhere has this been truer than with sexual abuse. While we now know that adults have always sexually abused children, the revelation came as a shock to Anglo-Saxon society in the 60s and 70s. It was in America and then Britain where academics such as Finkelhor (Horwath, 2010, p 261) began to open the door on the realities of sexual abuse.

It was inevitable that once child abuse had been discovered we would look for causes and abusers. Two doctrines arose: the feminist and the child protectionist (Jenks, 2001). The feminist view is that child abuse, like domestic violence against women, is committed more or less exclusively by men against vulnerable children. Abuse is an act of gender power and anger as much as anything else. When women committed abuse it was because they were forced to do so by men or placed in such a position by male dominance that they had no choice. The child protectionist view was that child abuse was a result of family dysfunction, this second view being seized upon by the right to demonstrate the loss of family values. In general, the government has taken the second view and the legislation, policy and procedures we find ourselves with today are based on this premise.

In our more enlightened society people may take it for granted that things are better for children than they were in the past, but as Pollock and Maitlock (cited in Bainham and Cretney, 1993) point out, too many professionals working with children still have to spend much of their time protecting children from intolerable situations rather than further improving tolerable situations for them. Indeed there is much debate about the lack of resources within child welfare and protection services that means we cannot do enough preventative work, but rather arrive after the damage is done.

Parents struggle to do what is right. We have already discussed the contradictory nature of the advice that is given. There is anxiety as to whether contemporary families can provide a sufficiently stable setting for children's healthy development matched by the fear of the risks the child may be at in the wider community. Despite fears about the stranger, child abuse remains firmly seated within the family. Since 2000 we have had the tragic deaths of Victoria Climbié, Peter Connelly and Daniel Pelka, amongst others; these children were killed by adults they should have been able to trust and in each case the agencies that might have been expected to protect them failed to do so. In response, social workers and other agencies are scapegoated and the government responds with new legislation, policy and procedures reflecting the child protection industry that continues to grow.

In January 2003, Lord Laming published his report into the death of Victoria Climbié, which found that health, police and social services missed 12 opportunities to save her. The inquiry that inevitably followed and subsequent legislation have recommended a raft of proposals. In 2008 was the death of Peter Donnelly and a second Laming Report once again followed with further change. In 2013 came the death of Daniel Polka and it is likely there will be further changes. Each tragedy brings with it another enquiry and further revisions to structures and systems that may or may not improve the way in which children are protected. In all these enquiries two things stand out: the importance that workers recognise and act upon concerns and that agencies communicate with each other.

What is abuse?

In some cases the answer to this question is obvious and straightforward. A bruise, a broken bone, a burn are all potential signs of abuse, but a withdrawn child, a thin child or a smelly child are not necessarily so. It is important to consider possible signs and symptoms in context and to not make assumptions either way. We know, for instance, that all young children get bruises, but where? A bruise on the shin is understandable, but one between the thighs or about the head is less so. Professionals need to observe, think and act if necessary. This is why recording any concern is vitally important and sharing these concerns with immediate colleagues or allied workers from other agencies is so important. Building a picture around the child allows professionals to make an informed judgement about a child and her possible needs.

Officially there are four types of abuse, as follows.

- Physical abuse: this includes hitting, kicking, beating, shaking and throwing, whether it causes bruises, broken bones or death.

- Sexual abuse: this is where children are forced or persuaded to perform sexual acts by others, whether that's looking at pornography, being touched sexually or actually having sex.

- Emotional abuse: when children are deprived of love and acceptance from their parents or guardians. They may be screamed at, blamed for things that aren't their fault and/or told they are worthless by their carers.

- Neglect: when parents or guardians do not provide the child with the required food, warmth, shelter, care and protection.

These labels are simply that and are useful for administrative purposes but no incident of abuse can simply be placed under one of these headings. For instance, sexual abuse is also emotionally abusing and probably physically abusing as well, neglect is also emotionally abusing and so forth. Abuse is complex both in relation to why and what has happened and in terms of investigation and outcomes. This is where accurate and child-centred assessment comes in to make certain that all the information is collected, collated and analysed. An important assessment gauge is what is called significant harm and is included in the Children Act 1989. The idea behind it is simple: is the harm the child is suffering significant to them? Shaking a baby is life-threatening, but shaking a twelve-year-old is probably not. Not feeding a ten-year-old is neglectful, but not feeding a teenager... and so on. We have to remember when applying significant harm that if a child has special needs then this may leave them more vulnerable, and we know that disabled child often suffer abuse that is not detected.

CASE STUDY

Daniel Pelka

Daniel Pelka suffered severe physical abuse and neglect at the hands of his mother Magdalena Luczak and her partner Mariusz Krezolek. He was tortured and neglected emotionally and physically. He was not fed and was inevitably undernourished and very thin, but professionals at the primary school he attended did not see what was happening. They were fooled by Daniel's carers. The couple deliberately spun a web of lies to cover up the abuse and, it has to be said, skilfully evaded any help they were offered. In this way they aped the behaviour of Peter Connelly's mother and her partner. Yet unlike Peter, Daniel was at school and observed by professionals. Other agencies also failed to act. Daniel died in April 2012 and in July 2013 both Magdalena Luczak and Mariusz Krezolek were sent to prison for life for his murder.

The Daniel Pelka case is tragic and highlights the need for practitioners not only to be aware of how a child is behaving, how they look and change, but also to make certain they are listening to what carers are saying and asking *Does it make sense?* There is a responsibility of all practitioners working with children to take an interest and if necessary to be inquisitive. This may make the professional feel uncomfortable, but it has to be done if we are to protect children. Practitioners also need to accept and understand the nature of abuse and there is no abuser template. Abusers come in all shapes and sizes, men and women, from all levels of society and employment.

Critical reflection

A student recently told me that someone she had known for a long time had been arrested for having indecent photographs of children on his computer. She was shocked as he did not seem like that sort of person.

» Reflect on your own views about those who abuse children. Do you have stereotypical attitudes?

Impact of abuse on development

As we have seen during the course of this book, and in particular with some of the case studies such as those on Yon, Terry, Sophie and Daniel, we know what can happen when a child does not receive the type of sensitive and loving care needed to stimulate physical and psychological growth. Early childhood development is shaped as much by negative experiences as by positive and while it is important, if a child is to build resilience, to experience challenges, abuse is something apart. Resilience is something we develop as we grow, starting from the early years and developing in order to allow us to deal with the stress and pressures that life presents. We can ask an interesting question here. Do we protect children in challenging situations, possibly removing the risk, or do we help them become resilient so they can deal with adversity? It is easy to argue that children should walk to school or get the bus, rather than being driven, but if you live in poverty do we equip the child to deal with the reality of the poverty they live in or protect them from it?

As we have discussed above, the nature and impact of abuse can be open to debate, for instance depending on the child's age and the culture in which the child lives. Serious non-accidental physical abuse, broken limbs, bruises, burns and so forth are clearly abusive and can have a long-term impact upon a child's development. They can lead to the child being disabled or even dying and they can lead to psychological problems, for instance in relation to trust. Children who receive loving care are likely to develop secure and appropriate attachments and positive internal working models, while those whose interactions with their caregivers are negative may develop insecure attachments and see themselves as neither loved nor loveable. Children who experience long-term emotional neglect or regular physical punishment will react as any animal might through fleeing or freezing.

Children in their early years are especially vulnerable to all forms of abuse and it can have long-term effects on their development. Physical abuse and neglect can cause long-term problems, but so can emotional neglect as we have seen with the discussion on brain development. Children who experience their caregivers as frightening or dangerous may develop disorganised attachments. They may be fearful of approaching their caregivers because they cannot predict whether they will be shouted at or cuddled. These children develop highly negative internal working models and see other people as not to be trusted, or may seek physical warmth from people they hardly know. Because their caregivers are unable to respond appropriately to their basic needs, these children may experience persistent and chronic stress. In the same way that the unborn can experience stress in the womb, the infant can as well, resulting in the brain being flooded by cortisol for prolonged periods that can have serious consequences. In previous case studies, in particular Terry and Yon, we saw how emotional abuse or neglect can have a significant impact not only on the child's psychological development but also on his physical growth. It is important to remind ourselves that while both Terry and Yon grew up in neglectful environments that were obvious, neglect and the impact it can have will happen in what appear to be the best of homes.

CASE STUDY

George

Connie was a nurse married to a GP. She had recently given birth to a son George, but the health visitor recognised he was struggling to put on any weight. He was referred to paediatric outpatients. While George and Connie were waiting, Connie decided to give George a bottle. An experienced nurse walked by and noticed the feed appeared thin. She mentioned this to the paediatrician due to see George.

It was established that Connie was deliberately giving George thin feeds. Social services and the police were called in and it became apparent that this was a case of fabricated illness, formerly Munchausen by proxy. The police applied a caution to the mother which had the consequence, as it was against a child, of meaning she could not work as a nurse in the future.

George was removed into foster care while a protection plan was put in place. This included therapy for Connie, agreement by his father to be the primary carer and regular visits from professionals.

If George had continued to receive inadequate nourishment, especially at such a young and vulnerable age, his long-term development would have been significantly affected, highlighting the need for early intervention.

Early intervention

Babies and toddlers are especially vulnerable to abuse and neglect. The significance of shaking, hitting, not feeding or emotionally neglecting an infant can be life-threatening or permanently debilitating. It is vital that practitioners understand the signs and symptoms of abuse and learn how to recognise them, have robust policy and procedures in place and have the courage to follow them in order to protect the child. I use the word 'courage' quite deliberately because we have to recognise that it is not always easy to raise concerns or make a referral. The worker may have got to know the family, to like them, and may fear repercussions should they report concerns. The worker may be sceptical about how effective social workers may be or may distrust social services and the police. Sometimes workers will minimise the evidence they are seeing, even hope the problem will go away. While these feelings are understandable, appropriate and regular training, team discussions and a generally positive approach to safeguarding within the setting will help the worker develop an appropriately robust attitude.

There is a fundamental dilemma for all of us involved in childcare and child protection and that concerns the point at which we should intervene. Previously in the book I have raised issues around parental choice and state intervention. For instance, in Scotland it is now against the law to smack a child at all, while in England and Wales you can smack within reason. Should the government be getting involved in this? Of course the state needs and must get involved when the abuse is serious, but where do we draw the line? When is state intervention appropriate and when is it not? Social services in England and Wales are increasingly becoming involved where children are obese, to the point of removing children from their parents. Is this a child protection or health issue? At the same time social workers know that if they get it wrong they may be castigated in the media. There was a cartoon in one of the social work journals with two identical pictures of a social worker being hung by a mob from a tree. Under one the legend said: *This is the social worker who did not take the child away* and under the second it read *This is the social worker who took the child away*.

Ideally we would live in a society in which families were being supported by services that worked alongside families in need and enabled them to improve their parenting without the need for intrusive intervention or court action. Lifting families out of poverty, providing practical education on being a parent and targeting benefits could eradicate much of the abuse and neglect we currently see arriving at the door of social services. This would allow social services to concentrate on the comparatively small number of very serious situations, for instance in the case of Daniel Pelka. The prevention v protection debate has raged for many years and will continue to do so until society can focus on the underlying causes of neglect. This will not take away those who deliberately abuse children and work to cover it up.

Despite the above it is clear that early intervention, especially with young children, is vitally important. One cannot afford to allow a young child to drift in neglectful or abusive conditions because we know that that child's development will be affected for life, but without supportive preventative services being readily available removal is often the only action available to them. Clearly when it comes to brain development early intervention with a family where a child is experiencing abuse or neglect is vitally important. While it is possible to repair some of the damage caused to the brain by early emotional neglect the repair will never be complete and the child will carry some degree of damage into adulthood.

In both the Victoria Climbié and Daniel Pelka cases there were cultural issues that inhibited practitioners' involvement, either because of language difficulties or through a fear that they would offend cultural niceties. The 2012 case of the abuse ring in Oxford that involved Asian men and vulnerable white girls also highlighted the fact that agencies can be reluctant to treat where there are cultural issues at play. It is, of course, important to acknowledge and respect cultural issues, but a child at risk of being abused is exactly that, whatever the cultural background. An extreme of this is genital mutilation and this type of abuse should never be tolerated and must be challenged and/or reported.

Inter-agency co-operation

Critical reflection

Before you read this section think about the various professionals involved in safeguarding and child protection.

» *How do you feel about social workers, teachers, police officers and health professionals?*

» *If you are already a childcare professional, how do you think others view you?*

Every agency that works with children has a role to play in safeguarding any child's welfare and an absolute obligation to report concerns. The document Working Together (2013) sets out the policy and procedures that agencies must follow and adhere to. As I have already highlighted, failings in inter-agency working and co-operation is often the reason children suffer. Social services will be the key agency in any child protection investigation. One of the first things that will happen when a referral comes in will be a strategy discussion with the police to decide who will take the referral. There are two options: a single agency investigation (police or social services); or a joint investigation with both agencies working together.

CASE STUDY

Sophie, Part 2

Sophie was the four-year-old daughter of Captain Louise and Duncan Hammon.

After calling social services due to a hand-shaped bruise found on Sophie's leg, the nursery worker went with Sophie and the social worker to the suite, a room like any sitting room within a police building. There were toys for Sophie to play with and juice and biscuits. Sophie would be interviewed by a specially trained social worker and police officer and the interview would be filmed and recorded. Photographs would be taken of the bruising and a decision might be made to have a police surgeon examine Sophie to see if she had other injuries.

Louise and Duncan Hammon would both be taken to the police station to be interviewed separately.

Once social services and the police have made a decision about who will work on a case, the information will be gathered from other agencies such as health, probation, education and the NSPCC. Working Together obliges agencies to share information about the child or other children within the immediate family. This is done to build up a contextual picture, for instance if there have been previous concerns.

Occasionally something will go wrong and a child will suffer abuse, further abuse or be placed at risk. Depending on the circumstances surrounding what happened there may be what is called a Serious Case Review (SCR), undertaken by an independent specialist and involving all the agencies and individuals that were involved in the case. During my career as a childcare and then child protection social worker I was involved in one such review. Quite simply the team I was part of had removed a child from its parents after A&E informed us that she had a spiral fracture of the left tibia. A spiral fracture comes about when the bone is twisted with great force and is likely to be evidence of a non-accidental injury. After undertaking checks we placed the child with the maternal grandmother rather than removing her into foster care. We organised supervised contact and the child was happy and well looked after. A week later an expert paediatrician reported to us that, after looking at X-rays and the rate of healing and calcium growth around the break, he estimated that the break could have occurred anything up to five days before the child was taken to A&E and that meant the maternal grandmother was in the timeline, as she had had care of the child during the period the injury might have occurred. We had to remove the child from the grandmother and place it in foster care. The Review took place and came to the conclusion that the child should have been placed in foster care from the beginning, or at least until all the evidence had been gathered. The Review was sympathetically conducted and talked of as a learning exercise, but that did not stop all of us involved feeling guilty and not a little ashamed. Reflection is essential in these circumstances and allows those involved to develop, improve and move on. Too often workers are blamed rather than being supported and helped to become better workers.

Critical reflection

Connie, in the case of George, and Louise, in the case of Sophie, are both professionals. Before you read on to find out what happens to Louise, how should we punish, restrict or label professionals that abuse their own children?

While it hits the headlines, the abuse of children by childcare professionals is actually very rare, but when it happens it causes grave concern for the public and other professionals. Teachers, social workers and police officers have all been prosecuted, but a case that startled the public and profession was the case of the female nursery worker who sexually abused very young children in her care and broadcast photographs of the abuse on the internet.

Little Ted's nursery

Society has got used to hearing about child death through neglect and abuse, the alleged failings of the practitioners that were there to protect and the parents that carried out the abuse. This is a trope of modern society, a repeating story that reflects the age in which we live, but despite this we can still be surprised and shocked. Surprising to the public and in many ways more chilling than some other events was the revelation in 2011 of sexual abuse taking place in the Little Ted's nursery in Plymouth. As the story broke we learned that between late 2008 and early 2009, Vanessa George, Colin Blanchard and Angela Allen met on Facebook and started to email and text message each other. The messages were often of a crude sexual nature. Police believe that the three were having a contest to see who could produce the most obscene picture. George started taking indecent pictures of two to five-year-old children attending Little Ted's, the nursery in which she worked. George, described in court as the *hub* of the ring, was given an indeterminate sentence with a minimum term of seven years for her role in the offences. A fourth member of the ring, Tracy Lyons of Portsmouth, pleaded guilty in March 2010 to assault of a child by penetration, sexual assault of a child under 13, causing a child under 13 to engage in sexual activity and three offences of distributing indecent photographs of a child. A fifth member of the ring, Tracy Dawber, also from Portsmouth, was found guilty of one count of sexually abusing a baby in October 2010.

Within this case there are four elements that in the public's mind at least set it apart from other cases. Firstly, the fact that we had not one, but three women sexually abusing very young children. We know that women sexually abuse, but it remains something that people struggle to comprehend. Women are meant to be caring, nurturing and loving. Secondly, Vanessa George, not the others, was a childcare practitioner charged with the ethical responsibility to care for vulnerable children. Practitioners have a duty of care for those in their charge and are expected, ethically and legally, to operate above and beyond what might be expected of anyone else. Thirdly, the abuse took place within a 'safe' setting. Fourthly, the use of technology and the virtual world for the discussion and planning of the abuse and the abuse itself.

A review was commissioned by Plymouth Safeguarding Children Board in June 2009 after the arrest of Vanessa George. As outlined above, SCRs are normally carried out by local safeguarding children boards when a serious incident or death of a child occurs, but given the extremely unusual circumstances, the focus of this review was on the nursery as a whole rather than individual children, and how the abuse could have taken place. SCR summaries are usually no more than half a dozen pages long but the executive summary of the Little Ted's review is 39 pages long, reflecting the nature of the issues, and it is detailed to enable the public, including the families affected, to understand as fully as possible its findings. The review looks at a range of factors around how the nursery was run, the supervision of staff, partnerships with families, accountability and safeguarding of children as well as the role of George within the nursery. It concludes that there was no indication *that any professional could have reasonably predicted that George might be a risk to children*, but does record a range of issues with the nursery management, culture and physical environment that meant safeguarding risks were not minimised. The report concluded that there were a number of lessons to be learned, for instance:

- In relation to mobile phones, the report says: *Whilst stopping staff carrying mobile phones is an important preventative measure and will mean that images cannot easily be transmitted electronically; this alone will not prevent abuse taking place* (6.4).

- An urgent need to develop effective staff supervision within early years settings (6.5).

- Staff did not recognise the escalation of George's sexualised behaviour as a warning sign and there is an urgent need for staff working in early years settings to receive training, to help recognise potential signs of abuse and become confident in responding to a fellow staff member's behaviour (6.9).

(www.plymouth.gov.uk/homepage/.../littletednurseryreview.html)

Critical questions

» *Who can we trust?*

» *How wary are you of men who work with young children?*

Working with families

In the majority of cases the child does not get removed from the family, they either remain in the home with support going in or it is the abuser that is removed. Everyone reading this will have a story to tell of where *they* (social services more often than not) *failed to do anything, did not do enough* or *allowed the child to be abused again*. We have already seen how agencies have failed some children, but in most cases positive action is taken to protect the child and where possible keep it within the family. Where social services often fail is not informing the other agencies what and why they are acting in the way they are. Whatever the outcome, practitioners, often the very practitioners that report concerns, will have to continue to work with the parents and family. One of the fears many workers have is how people will react after the investigation, after all the other agencies have gone away.

CASE STUDY

Sophie, Part 3

Louise Hammon admitted to hitting Sophie with the flat of her hand, but said it was the first time. She told the police she had felt differently towards Sophie since returning from Afghanistan. Duncan Hammon took time off work for a week while the agencies undertook an assessment and Louise remained in quarters on the base without having contact with Sophie. Duncan kept Sophie away from the nursery.

Louise accepted a police caution for hitting Sophie and faced further repercussions within the military. Sophie became subject to a child protection plan under physical abuse. The nursery manager and key worker went to the conference, both agreeing that Sophie was at risk. The parents refused to have any contact with the manager or worker during the meeting.

At the planning meeting, social services wanted Sophie to remain at the nursery, attending five mornings a week before going to her childminder each afternoon, but the parents wanted to find another nursery as *we have lost faith in them*.

The nursery manager recognised how important it was for Sophie to have a settled experience and how much she had enjoyed attending the nursery. She offered to meet with Sophie's parents away from the formality of the planning meeting and discuss why she and her staff had acted as they had and the benefits for Sophie of staying at the nursery. She added that if the parents still wanted to take Sophie away she would help them find a suitable new nursery.

Sophie remained at the nursery.

Honesty, clarity of purpose and keeping a focus on the needs of the child are vital, but when working with parents and families good social skills are essential to avoid conflict and resolve issues. It is also important to remain objective and reflect on how you might feel. If the child and abuser are remaining within the family and the abuser comes to the setting and wants to talk to you, how will you feel? If the abuse was serious, maybe sexual, overcoming your own anger or disgust at what has happened may be difficult and something you will have to talk through with a manager or colleague.

Practitioners working within the early years are required to contribute to child protection planning, attend meetings and liaise with other professionals. They may perform these tasks when a child who is at risk has left the early years setting or when a child who has been abused has early years siblings. In any involvement with a family where there is or may be child abuse the first thing is to make certain that you and any co-workers are safe at all times. This means following the organisation's health and safety procedures, making certain colleagues know where you are and what you are doing and that you follow your instincts. If you feel that something is not right, then it probably isn't and making yourself safe is important. Think about the Daniel Paluka case and how professionals involved with the parents report that they believed what was being said to them about Daniel was true. If you look at pictures of the couple (tattoos, piercings, etc), I also wonder if professionals were reluctant to risk challenging them. We all carry stereotypical views and what is important is that we do not let them cloud our judgement either by jumping to conclusions or being reluctant to challenge.

Critical reflection

Some sections of the media and the public call for all child abusers to be severely punished, but is punishment always the way forward? Should we not be considering rehabilitation to protect potential future victims? Rather than labelling and excluding offenders should we not be helping to integrate them back into society?

Conclusion

Child abuse will always be a difficult subject to explore because it can raise issues with us and challenge our own attitudes and beliefs. During the course of this chapter we have taken an overview of key issues for those working with the early years. We have discussed the dilemmas and pressures that professionals face when making decisions about children they are concerned about. We have followed the case of Sophie Hammon and how professionals worked together and with the family to protect her and to settle on a positive outcome for her. The idea of positive outcomes is what those of us working with children should focus on and that will often mean professionals being brave and stepping in to protect a child.

Summary

In this chapter we have discussed abuse and significant harm in respect to the nature of abuse, the importance of early intervention and the need to work in concert with other agencies. We also examined the challenges of working with a family in which there has been abuse.

Critical reflection

»   *Think about the childcare agencies you have worked with or been involved with. Have they operated a clear safeguarding/child protection policy?*

»   *Have we got our approach to protecting children right in Britain?*

Taking it further

Child abuse is a challenging subject to consider, but if we are to safeguard children we need to understand all aspects of it. We need to challenge ourselves. To do this you might explore the following:

The case reviews for both Little Ted's Nursery and Daniel Pelka are both available online:

www.coventrylscb.org.uk/dpelka.html

www.plymouth.gov.uk/homepage/.../littletednurseryreview.html

If you would like to read more then I would recommend:

Daniel, B, Wassell, S and Gilligan, R (2010) *Child Development for Child Care and Protection Workers*. London: Jessica Kingsley.

Ferguson, H (2011) *Child Protection Practice*. London: Palgrave.

Munro, E (2008) *Effective Child Protection*. London: SAGE.

O'Hagan, K (2006) *Identifying Emotional and Psychological Abuse*. Maidenhead: Open University Press.

Pritchard, C (2004) *The Child Abusers: Research and Controversy*. Maidenhead: Open University Press.

References

Bainham, A and Cretney, S (1993) *The Modern Law*. London: Sweet and Maxwell.

Department for Education (2013) Working Together to Safeguard Children. Available online at https://www.gov.uk/government/publications/working-together-to-safeguard-children (last accessed 2 June 2014).

Horwath, J (2010) *The Child's World*. London: Jessica Kingsley.

Humphries, L and Gully, T (1999) *Child Protection for Hospital-Based Practitioners*. London: WHURR.

Jenks, C (2001) *Childhood*. London: Routledge.

Kempe, C, Silverman, F, Steele, B, Droegemueller, W and Silver, H (1962) The Battered-Child Syndrome. *JAMA*, 181: 105–12.

8 Conclusion

Learning outcomes:

To reflect upon the key issues we have discussed during the course of this book and the importance of each of the following:

- theory and practice;
- the parent–child–practitioner relationship;
- government policy in the early years;
- protection and risk;
- conflicted children.

Introduction

In this conclusion I want to return to a number of key themes. Early years policy and practice has experienced a number of changes during recent years and the coming years promise to be just as challenging.

Discussion

Munro (2011), Nutbrown (2013) and others have highlighted the lack of theoretical understanding in relation to child development amongst some early years workers. The inability of a few workers to recognise when a child is being neglected, when they are not developing as they should or when there is abuse can have tragic consequences. We have seen this with the circumstances leading up to the death of Daniel Pelka; how 'obvious' signs were overlooked by practitioners. All practitioners should have a clear and comprehensive understanding of child development theory against which to observe and assess the children they come into contact with.

In the introduction I highlighted three theoretical themes that we would discuss during the course of this book. The first was continuity v discontinuity – whether a child's development is fluid and gradual or whether it occurs in stages. The easy answer is that both are true. In the chapter on foetal development we saw how the baby develops biologically in predictable stages in the womb, but once born, while biological development should continue, psychological and emotional development can happen in stages and are dependent on circumstances. This discussion has sought to answer questions such as *Do early childhood experiences predict future outcomes?* The answer is clearly yes.

The second theme concerned the active v passive child – whether individuals influence their own development through behaviour or whether individuals are at the mercy of their environment. The answer is both. As a subsiduary question we might ask: Do persons who experience the same event share the same developmental outcomes? Sometimes. These 'answers' are frustrating, but capture the essence of being human – that we are all different. Thirdly we have considered nature via nurture in order to explore how development is influenced by our innate biology and genetics (nature) yet moulded by our experiences (nurture). We have understood for a while that the quality of parenting can greatly influence a child's emotional and psychological development. We know that attachment, resilience and similar qualities develop early, but did not understand fully what was going on. Science has now given us epigenetics, the idea that care and even love can bring about genetic change offering further proof that the physical and psychological are integrated. We can therefore say that Bowlby was far more right than he could have possibly realised. Positive care and love does develop the life-long ability to develop and maintain positive attachments, not simply by influencing the psyche, but by changing our genetic makeup. It begins to explain why even identical twins can be emotionally different.

The parent–child–practitioner relationship

On several occasions during the course of this book we have discussed the value of building relationships and partnerships with parents that are designed to support and protect the child. As practitioners the onus is on us to initiate and build these partnerships and we need to ask the following inter-connected questions:

•   What do children and families want from us and our services?

•   What are the socio-economic and cultural barriers that have to be overcome for families to be able to work with us?

•   How do we engage families and stakeholders in changing and developing the services we offer?

By asking these and related questions we will gain a better understanding of what is needed to develop the partnership with individuals and groups, but it also gives us the chance as individual practitioners to reflect on our own attitudes. We all make subjective judgements, none of us are clear of discriminatory feelings and thoughts, but what is important in the early years practitioner is to be able to reflect and recognise these, and to make use of supervision to discuss how we are feeling.

CASE STUDY

Angela

Angela is an experienced nursery worker and has seen and dealt with many situations since she began her career. She has a BA in Early Childhood Studies and has the EYFS. In her own view she is mature and able to manage whatever comes along, but suddenly she is faced with something that she cannot cope with. Cindy is three and an intelligent, attractive child. There has recently been a Section 47 Child Protection investigation concerning Cindy and her new 'father' Gerry. There were concerns that Gerry had touched Cindy inappropriately, but neither the police nor social services could find any evidence to say that Cindy had suffered or was at risk of significant harm. Gerry now comes to collect Cindy and every time she watches him take the child away Angela feels a tremendous anger. Despite this she knows that for Cindy's sake she has to find a way to work with this situation and so she goes to see her supervisor.

Critical reflection

» *As her supervisor, what support and advice would you give Angela?*

While the above is an extreme case, situations like this will arise and will challenge the practitioner, but in order to support and protect children we have to find ways to work with even the most difficult of families. It is not discriminatory to have these feelings, but it is to not reflect and manage them in order to continue to provide a good service. Perhaps the most important thing is that workers at all levels are given the best possible training available and are obliged to take part in regular supervision.

Government policy in the early years

During the course of this book I have referred on several occasions to the tensions that exist between parental choice and government policy. Similar tensions exist between practitioners and the government. The coalition government have demonstrated a determination to move the early years agenda away from care with education towards a far more education-focused approach. I have alluded to my own preference for a Nordic approach in which the social development of the child is central, the idea that by crafting a well-rounded human being they are equipped to do better in education and in life generally. This said, I do not believe there is any significant appetite in Britain for what would be a social pedagogic approach. It is important, however, that practitioners, while accepting the government agenda, continue to work with children and families to improve social behaviour and inclusion wherever possible and in particular with hard-to-reach families.

The politics of early years provision is interesting and current, with all political parties taking an interest in the subject. The government is keen to get people into work to reduce the welfare budget and drive the economy, and parents, in particular mothers, remain central to that. Government recognises that childcare is very expensive for most working families and unless it is subsidised many cannot afford it, meaning that people either do not return to work or they seek help from relatives, particularly grandparents, to fill the gap. There is also a fundamental contradiction in government policy, as on the one hand they talk about the importance of family values and the need for children to have caring and settled home lives, and yet they need parents to work, which is something that can be disruptive for children. Successfully providing for good childcare and productive employment can be a challenge. Mothers will often seek out employment that fits around the child, but does not provide them with a fulfilling or well-paid experience. The government have made moves to encourage employers to be more flexible in employment arrangements and have improved paternity arrangements to help fathers play a more integrated role. Early years settings have also offered an expanding range of childcare opportunities including 24-hour provision.

Critical questions

» *Is it possible for parents to work and provide the child with everything it needs physically and emotionally?*

» *Should early years settings be available 24/7?*

» *What more could the government do?*

Protection and risk

On several occasions during this book I have highlighted concerns about our risk adverse society, be it a fear of the paedophile lurking on every street corner or the clump of nettles in the nursery garden. A butcher in Sudbury, Suffolk, was told to take down his display of game, including unskinned rabbits, because it might upset passing children; more like it would upset passing squeamish parents. I totally agree with Furedi (2008) that parents have become paranoid about the risks their children might face and, as I have argued, all children need to face risk in order to gain resilience and learn about the reality of life. We are of course talking about reasonable risk.

The problem we have as a society is that some children face serious risk, normally from adults that mean to do them harm. There have been a number of tragedies that might have been prevented. So what more can be done? We are dealing with system breakdown and human error, but also with problems and issues that are beyond the control of the agencies, such as poverty.

As a practitioner there are six principles of good practice to draw out from amongst many. In my opinion the first is by far the most important and I am often frustrated and bemused as to why practitioners who have chosen to enter a child-focused profession do not automatically follow it.

• First, as a childcare practitioner one has to be willing to get down with the child. One has to be willing to play with the child, talk and get dirty. Indeed this principle is simply good childcare practice.

• Second, individual regular supervision should be mandatory.

- Third, communication with all childcare colleagues is vital and professional responsibility must be maintained.

- Fourth, the child is paramount whatever the relationship with parents and whatever the culture.

- Fifth, practitioners have to think the unthinkable.

- Sixth, someone needs to be holding the baton, seeing the whole case, the patterns within it and how the evidence links together.

Fundamental to the above is the quality of training that is provided to all staff from the moment they step through the doors of the education establishment where they qualified (I recognise that not all childcare staff are qualified) and the agency or setting in which they are to work. There is, however, a clear and present danger in the amount of interference there is from central government. A new tragedy brings with it a new enquiry and further changes. No sooner have practitioners got used to one set of rules than a new set arrives.

Conclusion – conflicted parents and children

Through the revolutions in modern society, which continues to change rapidly, even children in the early years are living complex and pressurised lives. On the one side having these methods of communication and having access to limitless knowledge is wonderful, but it brings with it a dark threat to which many children have become victim. Parents want to do the right thing, they want to protect but allow access. The mobile phone can be seen as both a benefit and a danger to the child; the child can be contacted or call for help, but it can also be stolen, used to bully or to groom.

It is not only technology that brings conflict. Returning to Foucault and the body I am reminded that one can envisage the body as an unfinished biological and social project that we are continually tampering with, changing and adding things to. The more we know about our bodies, the more we are able to control, intervene and alter them, the more uncertain we become as to what the body actually is. The boundaries between the physical body and society are becoming increasingly blurred. It is a project carried on amid a profusion of reflexive resources: therapy and self-help manuals of all kinds, television programmes and magazine articles. Children today see the self as a project and this self-project is influenced by the media and what their peer groups say. Cyber bullying, peer exclusion and suicide are all products of children and young people suffering the consequences of not having the right body, the right look.

These conflicts are not only there for children, but also their parents. Despite, or perhaps because of these conflicts children and young people are increasingly pilots for the future and they cannot survive by following the routes of the past. They have become the fuel that feeds the development of society, the hope for the future, the future-makers. They have a chance to define their own future much more so than previous generations – whereas previous generations had the support of parents and a relatively clear map for the future, the current generation does not. And this has, of course, created new paths to explore for those of us who are involved in the development of early years learning and has left us with more questions than answers.

Summary

In this chapter I have sought to place child development into its modern context and highlighted key issues for now and the future. Childhood and parenting have changed dramatically during the last 30 years with scientific development, changing social attitudes, the spread of interactive technology and a new changing relationship with risk. We face an uncertain future in our work with children in the early years because of social, economic and political change. The most important thing for all practitioners is that we keep the child at the centre of our thinking in everything we do.

Critical reflection

» *Consider the future for children in the early years. What are the changes yet to come?*

» *Do these changes excite or scare you?*

At the very beginning of the introductory chapter to this book I wrote about my own childhood and some key influences. I suggested that I am very much a product of that upbringing. Take time to recall your own childhood and highlight the key influences from it. Then reflect upon the adult you are now.

» *How much has your childhood influenced the way you are now and what life events have altered you?*

References

Furedi, F (2008). *Paranoid Parenting: Why Ignoring the Experts May be Best for Your Child.* Chicago: Chicago Review Press.

Munro, E (2011) *The Munro Review of Child Protection: Final Report, A Child-Centred System.* Department of Education.

Nutbrown, C (2013) *Review of Early Education and Childcare Qualifications: Nutbrown Review Interim Report.* Department of Education.

Index